Beyond the Offering Plate : How to Build Wealth as a Believer

GORDON MILLS

Published by GORDON MILLS, 2024.

While every precaution has been taken in the preparation of this book, the publisher assumes no responsibility for errors or omissions, or for damages resulting from the use of the information contained herein.

BEYOND THE OFFERING PLATE : HOW TO BUILD WEALTH AS A BELIEVER

First edition. November 15, 2024.

Copyright © 2024 GORDON MILLS.

ISBN: 979-8230155904

Written by GORDON MILLS.

Table of Contents

.... 1
Opening Word 3
Introduction 6
Questions for Self-Reflection 9
Chapter 1 11
Rethinking Wealth as a Believer 12
Breaking the Poverty Mindset 13
Breaking the Chains of Poverty Thinking 16
Practical Steps to Break the Poverty Mindset 17
Reflection Questions 18
God's View on Wealth and Prosperity 19
God's View of Wealth: A Tool for Stewardship and Blessing 22
Practical Steps to Align Your Wealth with God's Purpose 23
Reflection Questions 24
Prosperity with Purpose 25
The Role of Generosity in Purpose-Driven Wealth 27
The Importance of a Kingdom-Focused Mindset 28
Practical Steps to Prosperity with Purpose 29
Chapter 2 31
Faith in Action – Building Wealth with Purpose 32
The Principle of Work and Diligence 33
The Discipline of Diligence 35
Faith in Action: Work and Diligence in Your Life 36
From Vision to Action: Creating a Financial Plan 38
Aligning Your Work with God's Calling 43
Reflection Questions 51
Budgeting as a Form of Stewardship 52
The Power of Budgeting for Financial Freedom 54
Saving and Investing for the Future 57
Avoiding Debt and Practicing Generosity 62
Chapter 3 68
Financial Literacy for Believers – Practical Skills for Wealth Building 69
Money Management and Wealth-Building Basics 70

Entrepreneurship and Creating Multiple Streams of Income 75
Planning for Retirement and Legacy Building.. 81
Chapter 4.. 86
The Hard Truth About Faith and Finances – Wisdom, Work, and Wealth 87
The Role of Tithing and Offering... 88
Why Faithful Tithers Sometimes Struggle Financially 89
Why Non-Tithers Sometimes Succeed Financially..................................... 91
Balancing Spiritual and Practical Principles 92
Your Financial Success Matters to God 93
Faith Without Action Leads to Frustration.. 96
The Danger of Religious Manipulation 98
The Success of Non-Believers.. 99
God's View on Financial Success..100
Breaking the Cycle of Financial Struggle...101
The Call to Wake Up 102
Chapter 5...104
Leaving a Legacy – Impacting Future Generations...................................105
Teaching the Next Generation about Faith and Finances........................106
Using Wealth to Transform Lives and Communities 111
Finishing Well – Living as a Testament of Faith and Financial Integrity 116
Chapter 6...122
Harnessing Technology for Wealth Building...123
Passive Income Strategies for the Digital Age 125
How I Attained Financial Independence 128
The Need for Mentorship on the Path to Financial Freedom..................135
Conclusion...140
Living a Balanced Life—Honoring God in Faith and Finances...............141
The Call to Live a Life of Purpose...142
Honoring God in Your Finances...144
Living with Intentionality 145
The Legacy You Leave..146
Reflection 149

BEYOND THE OFFERING Plate

How to Build Wealth as a Believer

GORDON MILLS

Beyond the Offering Plate
How to Build Wealth as a Believer

GORDON MILLS

Opening Word

How often have you heard that poverty is next to godliness? Or that the true Christian path requires avoiding financial success, focusing only on prayer and spiritual growth? These kinds of teachings, while well-meaning, have deceived many. For years, I believed that financial prosperity was somehow unholy—reserved for those who were worldly and disconnected from God's true calling. But as I began to study the scriptures, my perspective started to change.

You see, if we take a closer look at the Bible, we find a God who celebrates prosperity, who blesses hard work, and who encourages stewardship. From the story of Abraham, a man so wealthy that his riches became a symbol of God's covenant, to the teachings of Jesus Himself, who often used parables of investment, multiplication, and wealth, the Bible is far from dismissing material success. Instead, it shows that God desires His people to prosper—not just spiritually, but also in the physical realm.

But here's the catch: prosperity is not about seeking wealth for wealth's sake. No, that's not the point at all. The point is about understanding that wealth, when viewed through a God-centered lens, becomes a tool—an instrument for greater purposes. If you are a believer, then wealth is not your enemy; ignorance about what God truly desires for you is.

How many times have you heard someone say, "God wants me to be humble, so I shouldn't seek riches"? Or, "True believers live simply and should not desire wealth"? I used to believe that too. But I began asking myself: If God is the Creator of the universe, the one who owns the cattle on a thousand hills (Psalm 50:10), why would He want His children to struggle in poverty?

I know, I know, some of you are thinking: "But Jesus said it is harder for a rich man to enter the kingdom of God than for a camel to go through the eye of a needle." Yes, that's true. And it's a powerful reminder of the dangers of allowing wealth to become an idol. But here's the thing: the challenge isn't wealth itself—it's the **love** of money. Jesus was warning against greed, not the accumulation of resources for the good of the kingdom. You see, the issue isn't having wealth, but having wealth own you. The issue is where your heart is.

What if the true barrier between you and a life of abundance isn't God's will, but a misunderstanding of what He desires for you? What if you've been taught to avoid financial success because you thought it would compromise your faith? What if you've been convinced that wealth is inherently evil, when in fact it is one of the most powerful tools God can use to expand His kingdom and bless others?

I'm going to challenge you to think differently, to look beyond the offering plate, beyond the pulpit's call for tithes and offerings, and begin to see your financial potential as part of your divine calling. God isn't opposed to wealth. He's opposed to the love of money, the pursuit of wealth for selfish reasons, and the neglect of our responsibilities as stewards. There is a difference between the accumulation of wealth for self-glorification and the creation of wealth to serve others and advance the kingdom of God.

Consider this: In the early church, as described in the book of Acts, there were "no needy persons among them" (Acts 4:34). Why? Because they understood the power of community, stewardship, and shared resources. They worked together, built businesses together, and lived out the principles of prosperity and generosity. Imagine if we, as believers, embraced this same mindset today—what could we accomplish in our communities, in our churches, and in the world? What could we do for the Kingdom of God if we had financial freedom and were able to use our resources to further the gospel, feed the hungry, educate the poor, and empower the next generation?

Now, I know what you're thinking: "But Gordon, that's easy for you to say. You've figured it out. You've built wealth. But I'm stuck." Trust me, I've been there. I've spent years struggling with this same mindset, believing that wealth was something that belonged to the secular world, that it was beyond my reach or perhaps incompatible with my faith. But the truth is, I was wrong. I was standing in my own way, convincing myself that wealth was a barrier to spiritual growth when, in fact, it was an opportunity for growth.

I've written this book not just to challenge your understanding of wealth, but to give you a practical framework for creating wealth while remaining deeply rooted in your faith. I want to help you understand that it's not only possible to be financially prosperous and spiritually faithful, but it is also **necessary** for fulfilling the purpose God has for you.

Throughout these pages, we will explore the biblical foundations of wealth, from the principles of hard work and stewardship to the importance of generosity and investment. I'll share stories of believers who have done it—who have built wealth in a way that honors God, serves their communities, and impacts the world. You'll learn practical steps to take in your own life to break free from the chains of financial insecurity and step into a future where you can live abundantly.

But this is about more than just money. This is about changing the way we think about prosperity, work, and success. It's about understanding that being financially successful is not a contradiction to being a devout believer. In fact, it can be a testimony of God's goodness and provision. You can be both wealthy and godly. You can be financially independent and still honor God with every part of your life.

So let's begin this journey together. Let's break free from the lies and limitations that have held us back for so long. Let's move beyond the offering plate and embrace the fullness of what God has for us—not just spiritually, but in every area of our lives, including our finances. Are you ready to step into the life of abundance that God has promised? Because it's waiting for you. The question is: Are you ready to claim it?

The time to start building wealth as a believer is now.

Introduction

How many times have you heard that "money is the root of all evil" or that "God prefers us to be poor so we can focus on the kingdom"? I'm sure you've heard it. You've probably even believed it at one point, just like I did. For years, I believed that wealth and Christianity didn't mix, that being financially successful would somehow pull me away from God's will. I was raised in an environment where the pursuit of financial success was seen as worldly—a distraction from the true calling of believers.

But one day, as I sat in church, listening to the same old messages about "giving until it hurts" and "praying for God to provide," I felt something stirring in me—a question, a realization: **Is God really opposed to financial success?** And if not, why are so many believers struggling with poverty, financial stress, and insecurity? Could it be that there's something we're missing?

As I began to study the Bible more deeply, I came to a startling conclusion: The Bible is full of stories about people who were not only faithful, but also incredibly prosperous. From Abraham to Solomon, God blessed His people with wealth, and He didn't see this as a sign of disfavor. In fact, God's view of wealth is far more positive than many of us have been taught to believe.

Look at the story of Abraham, for instance. He wasn't just a man of faith; he was also a very wealthy man. In Genesis 13:2, it says, "Abram had become very wealthy in livestock and in silver and gold." God made a covenant with him, but He also made him prosperous. Why? Because wealth in Abraham's life wasn't just for personal luxury—it was a tool for the fulfillment of God's purpose. Abraham used his wealth to build a legacy, to help others, and to honor God.

Then we have Solomon, who, when asked by God what he wanted, didn't ask for riches or power, but for wisdom. Yet, God still gave him wealth beyond measure (1 Kings 3:13). God didn't rebuke Solomon for desiring wisdom, and

He didn't condemn Solomon for becoming rich. Instead, He saw Solomon's wealth as a blessing—one that could be used to do great things for the kingdom of God.

But what about Jesus? Doesn't He warn us that "it is easier for a camel to go through the eye of a needle than for a rich man to enter the kingdom of God" (Mark 10:25)? Yes, He did. But Jesus wasn't condemning wealth—He was warning against the **love** of money. There's a huge difference. In 1 Timothy 6:10, Paul says, "For the love of money is the root of all evil." It's not money itself that is evil—it's the obsession with it, the greed that comes when we make wealth our god. Jesus' warning wasn't about being wealthy, but about allowing wealth to dominate your heart and mind.

Now, I'm not saying that money should be your focus or that you should be obsessed with becoming rich. But what I want to challenge you with in this book is this: *God is not against you being financially successful*. In fact, He wants to bless you, not only spiritually but also materially, so that you can be a blessing to others. God wants you to live in abundance, not just for your own sake, but so that you can advance His kingdom on earth.

But there's a catch. We've been taught for so long to be passive when it comes to finances. We've been told that God will provide for us, so we don't need to worry about how to make money or how to grow it. We've been told to pray, give our tithes, and wait for God's miracle. While there's truth in trusting God to provide, there's also a responsibility on our part. You see, God doesn't perform magic. He blesses those who put in the work, those who are good stewards of their resources, and those who are willing to take responsibility for their financial future.

Now, let me share this—one that's a bit closer to home. I'll be transparent with you: there was a time in my life when I was struggling financially, even though I was a believer. I had the same mentality that many Christians have: "If I just pray enough, God will provide." But after years of barely making ends meet, I realized that I wasn't doing my part. I wasn't being a good steward of the resources God had given me.

It was then that I decided to take action. I started learning about business, investing, and how to create multiple streams of income. I prayed, yes, but I also worked hard, stayed disciplined, and sought wisdom from others who had successfully built wealth. Over time, my financial situation changed. I'm not saying this to boast—I'm telling you this because I want you to understand that you too can build wealth while keeping your faith strong. It's not about having a "get rich quick" mentality; it's about aligning your work with God's purpose for your life and being diligent in everything you do.

You see, wealth is a tool, not the goal. The ultimate goal is to serve God and others. But in order to serve effectively, you need resources. Imagine what you could do if you had the financial freedom to help others, to support your church, to fund mission work, to send your children to school, or to create jobs for those in your community. Wealth, when used correctly, can be a powerful tool for the advancement of God's kingdom.

In the coming chapters, we'll explore the practical steps you can take to build wealth as a believer. We'll dive into biblical principles of stewardship, hard work, and generosity, and we'll look at how you can transform your mindset about money.

I believe that God wants you to prosper, not for selfish reasons, but so that you can be a blessing to others. It's time for us to stop seeing wealth as a curse and start viewing it as a tool for God's glory. If you're ready to take the first step toward building wealth and honoring God with your finances, then let's begin. The journey starts here, and I'm excited to walk with you every step of the way.

Questions for Self-Reflection

1. How often have you believed that financial success and faith in God can't go hand-in-hand? What messages have you heard in church or from others that reinforced this belief?

2. Have you ever felt guilty for wanting to achieve financial success? Do you believe that desiring wealth makes you less godly or distracted from God's calling?

3. How do you currently view wealth? Do you see it as a tool for God's kingdom or as something to avoid altogether? How has this view affected your financial decisions?

4. What if the barrier between you and a life of abundance isn't God's will, but a misunderstanding of His desire for you? How might your life change if you viewed financial success as something God wants for you, not against you?

5. In what areas of your life are you actively taking responsibility for your financial future? Are there steps you can take today to become more diligent with the resources God has entrusted to you?

6. Do you believe that God rewards hard work, diligence, and good stewardship? How does this belief shape your attitude toward your job, your investments, or your financial habits?

7. When was the last time you prayed for financial wisdom? What practical steps can you take today to start learning about managing money in a way that honors God?

8. Do you know people around you—perhaps even in your church—who have successfully built wealth while staying true to their faith? What can you learn from their stories, and how can you apply those lessons to your own life?

9. How do you define "success" in your life? Is it simply about material wealth, or do you consider factors like faithfulness, generosity, and fulfilling God's purpose in your life as key components of true success?

10. Are you currently waiting for a financial miracle, or are you actively working toward financial freedom through hard work, discipline, and stewardship? How might your approach to money change if you combined both faith and action?

11. How can building wealth in a godly way impact your ability to serve others? What opportunities could arise if you had the financial resources to help your family, support your church, or fund charitable causes?

12. Have you ever thought of wealth as a tool for the advancement of God's kingdom? What would it look like if your financial resources were used to further God's work on earth?

13. What limiting beliefs do you hold about money that may be hindering your progress toward financial abundance? How can you reframe these beliefs to align with what Scripture says about God's provision and blessings?

14. How would your financial situation change if you truly believed that God is not opposed to your prosperity, but rather wants you to prosper and succeed for His glory?

15. If you had the financial freedom to make a difference in your community or to support your church in significant ways, how would that change your perspective on wealth?

These questions are designed to help you pause and reflect on your current understanding of wealth, faith, and your financial journey. By answering them honestly, you can begin to break free from limiting beliefs and start embracing a mindset that allows you to build wealth while honoring God.

Chapter 1

Rethinking Wealth as a Believer

Breaking the Poverty Mindset

Many of us have heard it time and time again: "Poverty is next to godliness." Some preachers might say that a poor life is a life of humility, or worse, that financial struggles are a sign of God's favor. But what if I told you that this mindset is not only wrong but can also hold you back from the abundance God truly desires for you?

As believers, it's easy to fall into the trap of thinking that being wealthy somehow makes you less godly. After all, didn't Jesus say that it's harder for a rich man to enter the kingdom of God than for a camel to go through the eye of a needle? (Matthew 19:24). Yes, Jesus did speak about the dangers of wealth when it becomes an idol, but He didn't say that wealth, in and of itself, is evil.

Let's take a step back and think about it. The problem isn't wealth—it's our **view** of wealth. For many, the idea of accumulating wealth while maintaining strong faith in God seems like a contradiction. We are taught that wealth is inherently sinful, and that a person who lives a life of abundance is somehow more distant from God. But if you look at the Bible with fresh eyes, you'll see a very different picture.

God is the Creator of everything. He created the heavens, the earth, and everything in it (Genesis 1:1). God is not against prosperity; in fact, He wants us to thrive. His promises for His people are full of abundance and blessings. But how did we get so far off track? Why do so many believers struggle with the idea of wealth, especially when it comes to reconciling it with their faith?

Poverty and Godliness: A Misunderstanding

In the past, many churches taught that poverty was a sign of holiness. It was almost as if the less you had, the more spiritually mature you were. There's no denying that Jesus warned against greed, and He did say in Matthew 6:24, **"You cannot serve both God and money."** But nowhere in the Bible does it say that having money or wealth is inherently sinful.

It's important to remember that some of the most faithful people in the Bible were wealthy. Take Abraham, for instance. Abraham was a man of great faith and wealth (Genesis 13:2). God didn't condemn him for his wealth. In fact, God blessed him and made him the father of many nations. If we look at the lives of Solomon, Job, and even David, we see that wealth and godliness can go hand-in-hand when managed correctly.

But here's the catch: prosperity isn't just about acquiring material goods—it's about using what God has given you for His glory. If you've been blessed with wealth, your responsibility is to steward it well, bless others, and support the kingdom of God. But if we buy into the lie that wealth is bad, we might miss out on the very tools God wants to use to fulfill His purpose in our lives.

The Danger of the Poverty Mindset

So, why does this poverty mindset exist, and why is it so dangerous for believers? The poverty mindset is based on the idea that money is bad, that wealth corrupts, or that financial prosperity is a sign of spiritual failure. This thinking can be deeply rooted in cultural beliefs, church teachings, or even family backgrounds.

I've seen it firsthand, not only in the church but also in my own community. Many people grow up believing that striving for wealth is selfish or greedy. They're taught that the pursuit of money is somehow incompatible with their relationship with God. But in truth, this mindset only creates a cycle of limitation. If you think you're supposed to be poor or struggle financially as a believer, then you'll never take the necessary steps to create financial abundance in your life.

This kind of thinking holds you back from seeing opportunities to create wealth and provides a false sense of security in mediocrity. It prevents you from asking the right questions: **Why can't I be financially successful and serve God? Why can't I provide for my family, grow my business, and bless others with the resources God has given me?** The poverty mindset keeps you in survival mode rather than thriving mode.

I know of many individuals who have broken free from this cycle. One of my close friends, Dmitri, grew up in a church that taught that money was evil. He struggled with his faith for years, believing that working hard to make money would take him further away from God. It wasn't until he realized that he could use his skills to help others that he began to change his mindset. Today, Dmitri is a successful entrepreneur who uses his wealth to fund church projects, sponsor underprivileged children, and support local communities. His faith has only grown stronger as he embraces the abundance God has given him.

The Biblical View of Wealth

So, where does this leave us? What is the truth about wealth according to the Bible?

First, let's remember that God is not opposed to wealth. He actually provides for His children in abundance. Psalm 23:1 says, *"The Lord is my shepherd; I lack nothing."* In Deuteronomy 8:18, God reminds us, *"But remember the Lord your God, for it is He who gives you the ability to produce wealth."* This is a reminder that God wants His people to prosper. It is He who gives us the ability to create wealth.

God's plan for your life is not to leave you struggling in poverty but to use the resources He has given you to fulfill your purpose. Proverbs 10:22 says, *"The blessing of the Lord brings wealth, without painful toil for it."* This is a promise that when we trust in God and follow His principles, He will bless us. But this doesn't mean that wealth will come without effort—rather, it's about understanding that the work you do, the business you build, and the efforts you put in are all ways God can bless you. You don't have to feel guilty for building wealth as long as you honor God in the process.

It's also worth noting that God warns us about the dangers of **loving money**. 1 Timothy 6:10 states, **"For the love of money is the root of all evil."** Wealth itself is not the problem—it's when we begin to place our trust in money rather than in God. The key is to keep money in its proper place: as a tool to serve God's purposes, not as an idol to be worshiped.

Breaking the Chains of Poverty Thinking

Now, let me share a bit about my own story. Growing up, I didn't have much. My family struggled financially, and I carried a mindset that money was something to be avoided if I wanted to please God. But as I began to study the Scriptures more deeply and understand God's promises of provision, I realized that I was limiting myself.

One of the key turning points came when I began to see how God used people of wealth in the Bible to advance His kingdom. Abraham, Job, David—these men of faith were blessed with wealth, but they didn't hoard it. They used their resources to serve others, build the kingdom of God, and bless those around them.

I started to break free from that poverty mindset by taking small steps: I started learning about personal finance, investing, and entrepreneurship. And yes, I also began to pray for wisdom in these areas. As I followed God's leading and acted on the opportunities He brought me, my financial situation began to change.

Today, I am not only financially free but also in a position to give back—something I never thought possible in my earlier years. My wealth is a tool, not a burden. It enables me to provide for my family, invest in my community, and fund the work of the kingdom. And I do all this while remaining fully committed to my faith.

Practical Steps to Break the Poverty Mindset

Here's how you can start breaking free from the poverty mindset and begin building wealth that honors God:

1. **Renew your mind:** Begin by understanding that God desires for you to prosper. Read Scriptures like Deuteronomy 8:18, Proverbs 10:22, and 1 Timothy 6:10. Memorize them, meditate on them, and let them change how you view money.

2. **Start with small steps**: Take control of your finances today. Create a budget, set financial goals, and track your progress. Don't wait for a miracle—take action now.

3. **Seek knowledge**: Educate yourself on personal finance, investing, and entrepreneurship. There's no shame in learning how to manage wealth. The more you know, the better equipped you'll be to handle God's blessings.

4. **Pray for wisdom**: Ask God to guide you in your financial decisions. James 1:5 promises, "If any of you lacks wisdom, let him ask of God, who gives to all liberally and without reproach." Trust God to provide you with the insights you need.

Reflection Questions

What limiting beliefs about wealth have you been holding on to? How can you replace them with God's truth?

- How do you view wealth now? Do you see it as a tool for God's kingdom, or do you still struggle with guilt around having money?

- What small steps can you take today to break free from the poverty mindset and begin building wealth God's way?

Don't allow the lie that poverty equals godliness to hold you back. God has more for you. Take that first step toward breaking free from the chains of poverty thinking, and watch how He will use your wealth to fulfill His purpose in your life.

God's View on Wealth and Prosperity

As a believer, you've probably heard countless teachings on how we should handle our finances. Some might say that wealth is a blessing, while others claim it's a hindrance to our spiritual life. But what does the Bible truly say about wealth and prosperity? More importantly, how can you align your financial journey with God's will, without feeling guilty about it?

In this chapter, we'll look at the lives of some key biblical figures—Abraham, Job, and Lydia—who were prosperous, yet their wealth never stood in the way of their relationship with God. Rather, their wealth was a tool to advance God's kingdom and serve others. It's time to break free from the notion that wealth and faith are at odds with one another.

Let's begin by taking a deeper look at the lives of these figures.

Abraham: The Father of Faith and Wealth

Abraham's story is one that many believers are familiar with. He is known as the "father of faith," a man who trusted God even when things seemed impossible. But did you know that Abraham was also a wealthy man? In fact, he was incredibly prosperous.

Genesis 13:2 tells us, **"Abram had become very wealthy in livestock and in silver and gold."** We see here that God didn't just bless Abraham spiritually; He blessed him materially as well. Abraham's wealth didn't come through dishonest gain or selfish ambition. It came through God's blessing as he walked in faith.

Why is this important? Because Abraham didn't let his wealth distract him from his relationship with God. In fact, it was because of his faith that he was entrusted with such prosperity. He knew that his wealth was not for his own benefit but was a tool that God could use for His purposes. When God asked

Abraham to sacrifice his only son Isaac, Abraham's faith was so strong that he obeyed, trusting that God would provide. And provide He did—Abraham's obedience led to God's promises being fulfilled, both spiritually and materially (Genesis 22:15-18).

Abraham's wealth was not a sign of spiritual failure but a sign of God's favor and faithfulness. God blesses those who walk in faith, and that includes blessing them with resources that allow them to fulfill His purposes. Abraham's story teaches us that wealth and faith can go hand-in-hand when we put God first.

Job: A Man of Integrity in Prosperity and Adversity

JOB'S STORY IS ONE that demonstrates both the trials of life and the richness of God's blessings. Job was a man who had everything—wealth, family, and health. In fact, Job 1:3 says, **"He was the greatest man among all the people of the East."** But as you know, Job's life took a drastic turn when he lost everything. His wealth, his health, and even his children were taken away in an instant.

But here's the thing—Job never blamed God for his circumstances. In Job 1:21, he said, **"The Lord gave and the Lord has taken away; may the name of the Lord be praised."** Even in the midst of his losses, Job's faith remained unshaken. And when God eventually restored Job's fortunes, He gave him twice as much as he had before (Job 42:10).

What can we learn from Job's story? Wealth can be a blessing, but it is not the source of our security. Job's true security was in his relationship with God. Wealth may come and go, but our faith should remain firm. Job's prosperity wasn't an indication of his worth—it was simply a reflection of God's favor. And when God chose to take everything away, Job still trusted God, showing that true prosperity is not just about financial gain but about spiritual richness.

Job teaches us to put our faith in God, not in the things we own. Wealth is temporary, but faith is eternal. If we can learn to hold onto God in times of abundance and in times of loss, we will be able to walk in true prosperity.

Lydia: A Businesswoman with a Heart for God

Now, let's turn to Lydia, a lesser-known figure in the Bible but one who exemplifies a woman of wealth and faith. Lydia was a successful businesswoman who sold purple cloth, a luxury item that was in high demand (Acts 16:14). She was likely quite wealthy, yet her wealth did not cause her to become proud or self-reliant. Instead, Lydia used her success to serve God and advance His kingdom.

When Lydia encountered Paul, she didn't just listen to his teachings—she acted on them. Acts 16:15 says, *"When she and the members of her household were baptized, she invited us to her home."* Lydia's response was immediate. She understood that her wealth wasn't just for her own enjoyment but was a resource to serve God and support the work of the ministry. She used her home as a base for Paul's ministry and opened her doors to those in need.

Lydia's story shows us that prosperity doesn't have to be a barrier to faith. In fact, wealth can be a tool for serving others and advancing the kingdom of God. When we see our wealth as something to be used for God's purposes—whether it's providing for our family, supporting the church, or helping those in need—we can truly live out the principles of stewardship and generosity.

God's View of Wealth: A Tool for Stewardship and Blessing

So, what do we learn from the examples of Abraham, Job, and Lydia? The Bible doesn't condemn wealth; it teaches us how to use it wisely and for God's purposes. In 1 Timothy 6:17-19, Paul instructs believers to *"command those who are rich in this present world not to be arrogant nor to put their hope in wealth, which is so uncertain, but to put their hope in God, who richly provides us with everything for our enjoyment."* He continues, *"Command them to do good, to be rich in good deeds, and to be generous and willing to share."*

God's view of wealth is that it should be used for His glory, to bless others, and to provide for those in need. Wealth is not evil, but it can be a stumbling block if we place our trust in it instead of in God. The Bible calls us to be good stewards of the resources God has entrusted to us, using them to further His kingdom and serve others.

Practical Steps to Align Your Wealth with God's Purpose

Here's how you can begin to align your view of wealth with God's will:

1. **Change your perspective**: Start by recognizing that wealth is not inherently evil. The Bible encourages us to prosper, but we must ensure that our hearts remain focused on God, not on money itself.

2. **Practice generosity**: Look for ways to use your wealth to bless others. Whether it's giving to charity, supporting the church, or helping those in need, make generosity a priority in your life.

3. **Be a good steward**: Take responsibility for the resources God has given you. Create a budget, save, invest, and seek wisdom in managing your finances. When you handle your wealth wisely, you're showing God that He can trust you with more.

4. **Seek God's guidance**: Pray for wisdom in your financial decisions. Trust that God will lead you in how to use your wealth for His glory.

Reflection Questions

How do you view wealth in your life? Do you see it as a tool for God's kingdom or as something to be avoided?

- Are there any areas of your financial life where you feel convicted to act differently—whether it's practicing generosity, stewardship, or seeking God's guidance?

- How can you begin to use your wealth to serve others and advance God's kingdom?

Wealth is not about us—it's about what we do with it. Just like Abraham, Job, and Lydia, you can use your prosperity to honor God and bless others. Start today by changing your mindset, taking action, and trusting God to guide you in using your wealth for His purposes.

Prosperity with Purpose

So, we've talked about the importance of aligning your faith with your financial journey. We've looked at the biblical view on wealth and prosperity. Now, let's get to the heart of why prosperity is important—and why it shouldn't just be about stacking up money for the sake of it. Prosperity, when truly understood, is about purpose. It's not about how much wealth you can accumulate; it's about how you use the wealth you have to advance God's kingdom and help others.

Too often, we think of wealth as an end goal. We imagine the nice car, the big house, and the vacations to exotic places. But true prosperity with purpose is about using the blessings God has given you to serve others, build His kingdom, and bring glory to His name. Let's take a deeper look at this idea of prosperity with purpose, and why it's so important for believers like you and me to view wealth in this way.

The Foundation of Purpose-Driven Wealth

In the world, wealth is often seen as a symbol of status. We are bombarded by advertisements telling us that the more we buy, the happier we will be. But as a believer, we need to flip the script. Prosperity is not about what we can buy for ourselves; it's about what we can do with the resources God has entrusted to us. The Bible is clear about this—wealth is meant to be used for good, for service, and for the glory of God.

Proverbs 3:9-10 says, *"Honor the Lord with your wealth, with the firstfruits of all your crops; then your barns will be filled to overflowing, and your vats will brim over with new wine."* This isn't just about receiving blessings for yourself; it's about using what God has given you to honor Him. When you honor God with your wealth, you're acknowledging that it's not yours to keep for your own selfish purposes, but that it's a tool to be used for a greater good.

The Bible teaches us that wealth can serve a higher purpose, and that purpose is to further God's kingdom. That means using your financial resources to build churches, support missionaries, invest in education, care for the poor, and do whatever else God calls you to do with what He has blessed you with.

God's Purpose for Prosperity

The Bible speaks to us directly about the purpose of wealth, and it's important to understand that God's plan for prosperity is not just about us living comfortably. Deuteronomy 8:18 says, *"But remember the Lord your God, for it is he who gives you the ability to produce wealth, and so confirms his covenant, which he swore to your ancestors, as it is today."* God gives us the ability to produce wealth not for selfish gain but to fulfill His covenant and purpose.

In Matthew 6:33, Jesus reminds us, *"But seek first his kingdom and his righteousness, and all these things will be given to you as well."* When we put God's kingdom first, our wealth and resources fall into place. Prosperity with purpose means putting God's work ahead of our own desires and using what we have to help others. God promises that when we seek His kingdom, everything we need will be provided.

Jesus also spoke about the importance of stewardship. In the parable of the talents (Matthew 25:14-30), He highlights the importance of using what we've been given wisely. The servants who used their talents wisely were praised, while the one who buried his talent was reprimanded. The message is clear: God wants us to use our resources, including our wealth, to serve Him and multiply what He's given us.

The Role of Generosity in Purpose-Driven Wealth

One of the clearest ways to live out prosperity with purpose is through generosity. When we hold onto our wealth too tightly, it can become an idol in our lives. But when we practice generosity, we are releasing control and trusting God to provide. Proverbs 11:24-25 says, *"One person gives freely, yet gains even more; another withholds unduly, but comes to poverty. A generous person will prosper; whoever refreshes others will be refreshed."* Generosity is not just an act of kindness—it's a spiritual principle that aligns us with God's will.

True prosperity with purpose means using your wealth to bless others, not just to bless yourself. We are called to be conduits of God's blessings, not reservoirs. In 2 Corinthians 9:7, Paul writes, *"Each of you should give what you have decided in your heart to give, not reluctantly or under compulsion, for God loves a cheerful giver."* Generosity is a heart attitude. When we give freely and cheerfully, we are partnering with God to meet the needs of others and advance His kingdom.

As you look at your own life and financial situation, consider this question: How can you be more generous? How can you use your wealth to help others, support ministries, and bring glory to God?

The Importance of a Kingdom-Focused Mindset

To live with prosperity and purpose, we need to shift our mindset. We can't view wealth through the world's lens of accumulation for personal gain. Instead, we must view it as a tool to fulfill God's purposes in the earth. God has given us resources, talents, and opportunities, and He wants us to use them for His glory. We are called to be stewards, not hoarders, of the blessings we've received.

Matthew 25:34-36 tells us that when we serve others—feeding the hungry, clothing the naked, visiting the sick, and caring for the lonely—we are serving Jesus Himself. Our wealth and resources should be used in service to others, in building God's kingdom here on earth. This is the true purpose of prosperity: to make a difference and leave a lasting legacy.

Practical Steps to Prosperity with Purpose

So, how can you begin living with prosperity and purpose? Here are some practical steps to help you get started:

1. **Shift your mindset:** Start viewing your wealth as a tool for God's kingdom, not as a means to personal gain. Ask God to help you see opportunities to use your resources to bless others.

2. **Be generous:** Look for ways to be generous with your wealth. Give to your church, support missionaries, or help those in need. Practice generosity regularly, knowing that God loves a cheerful giver.

3. **Invest in God's work:** Consider how you can use your business, your investments, or your skills to advance God's kingdom. Whether it's supporting a ministry or helping someone in need, make sure your resources are used for eternal purposes.

4. **Seek God's guidance:** Always ask God how He wants you to use the blessings He has given you. He will direct your steps and show you how to align your wealth with His will.

Reflection Questions

- How do you view your wealth and resources? Are you focused on accumulation, or are you using them to serve others and advance God's kingdom?

- What are some ways you can start being more generous with your finances today?

- How can you shift your mindset to view prosperity as a tool for God's purposes, rather than a symbol of personal success?

Living with prosperity and purpose is about changing the way you think and use what God has given you. It's not just about accumulating wealth for personal gain, but using it to build the kingdom of God and bless others. Start today by shifting your mindset, being generous, and seeking God's guidance in everything you do. When you live with purpose, your wealth becomes a tool for eternal impact.

Chapter 2

Faith in Action – Building Wealth with Purpose

The Principle of Work and Diligence

Alright, now that we've laid the foundation for why prosperity with purpose matters, let's get down to the nitty-gritty of how you can build wealth in a way that honors God. There's no magic formula. If you want to create financial abundance that serves a greater purpose, there's one crucial principle you must embrace: work and diligence. Simply put, hard work isn't just a good idea—it's an essential element to seeing financial growth.

I know, some people might think, "I'll just pray, and God will send me a check in the mail," but that's not how it works. Faith and action go hand in hand. You can have faith that God will provide, but you also have to show up and put in the work. Proverbs 10:4 says it straight: *"Lazy hands make for poverty, but diligent hands bring wealth."* So, if you're sitting around waiting for a miracle without putting in any effort, you're missing the point. God honors hard work and diligence, and that's the first step toward building wealth with purpose.

Work: The Pathway to Prosperity

Work is not a punishment; it's a blessing. From the very beginning, God gave mankind the responsibility to work. In Genesis 2:15, we see that God placed Adam in the Garden of Eden "to work it and take care of it." Work is part of God's design for us, and it's through diligent work that we create value, serve others, and earn our living.

This isn't about working to the point of burnout, but about working with purpose, diligence, and excellence. Whether you're working a job, running a business, or freelancing, the way you approach your work matters.

You see, work brings structure, opportunity, and discipline into our lives. Through work, you gain the skills needed to succeed and grow in your field.

It's through consistent, diligent effort that you build momentum, unlock new opportunities, and begin to see your financial growth. And it doesn't have to be a glamorous job or business for God to bless it. Whatever you do, do it well and with excellence.

Look at Proverbs 12:11—*"Those who work their land will have abundant food, but those who chase fantasies have no sense."* This verse teaches us that success doesn't come from chasing quick fixes or shortcuts. Success comes from working diligently and staying focused on your goals. If you're constantly looking for the "easy way out," you'll find yourself stuck, with no real progress. But if you stick with the work, no matter how hard or tedious it seems, you will see fruit from your labor.

The Discipline of Diligence

Diligence is about doing your work well, not just quickly or efficiently. It's about giving your best in everything, day in and day out. In the same way a farmer tends to his crops with care, you must tend to your own work with the same attention to detail. This takes discipline, focus, and a mindset that says, "I am here to give my best, and I will do whatever it takes to honor God with the work He has entrusted to me."

Proverbs 13:4 reminds us of the importance of diligence: *"The sluggard craves and gets nothing, but the desires of the diligent are fully satisfied."* Notice the difference here: the sluggard craves, but gets nothing. The diligent person, however, sees their desires fulfilled. Why? Because they put in the effort and stayed the course. They understood that there's no shortcut to success. Diligence is the key.

When you're diligent in your work, God sees your effort. He rewards it. And sometimes, the rewards aren't just financial—they can be opportunities, promotions, relationships, and skills that add value to your life. God honors faithfulness in the small things. Luke 16:10 says, *"Whoever can be trusted with very little can also be trusted with much."* If you can show diligence and faithfulness in the small things, God will give you more to manage. You'll find that your financial growth comes from not just the size of your income, but your ability to handle what you have with wisdom and diligence.

Faith in Action: Work and Diligence in Your Life

It's one thing to talk about work and diligence, but it's another to put it into action. So, how can you live this out in your own life? Here are a few steps you can take:

1. **Set clear goals for your work:** What do you want to accomplish? Whether you're working a full-time job, running a business, or pursuing a passion project, set clear goals. Proverbs 21:5 says, *"The plans of the diligent lead to profit as surely as haste leads to poverty."* Be intentional with your work and stay focused on your goals.

2. **Commit to excellence:** Whatever you do, do it with all your heart. Proverbs 22:29 says, "Do you see someone skilled in their work? They will stand before kings; they will not stand before obscure men." Excellence leads to recognition, and it leads to opportunities.

3. **Be consistent:** Diligence is about consistency. Don't expect instant results. Keep showing up, keep working, and keep improving. Small steps over time will lead to big results.

4. **Work as if you're working for God**: Colossians 3:23 tells us, "Whatever you do, work at it with all your heart, as working for the Lord, not for human masters." This mindset will transform your work from just a job to a way of honoring God.

Reflection Questions

- Are you putting in the effort required to achieve your financial goals? How does your work reflect your faith and diligence?

- What areas of your work could you improve in terms of excellence and focus? What would happen if you started giving your best in everything you do?

- Do you see your work as a way to honor God? How can you shift your mindset to work with purpose and diligence?

Remember, wealth doesn't come from wishing or hoping—it comes from hard work, diligence, and the willingness to show up and give your best. This is where faith meets action. Trust God to provide, but also work diligently, knowing that He honors those who give their best. When you work with excellence, you're building not only your wealth but also your legacy and your purpose.

From Vision to Action: Creating a Financial Plan

Alright, now that we've talked about how work and diligence are essential to building wealth, it's time to take things a step further. We're going to talk about how to create a financial plan that aligns with your faith. This isn't just about numbers—it's about making sure that the way you manage your money reflects your values, priorities, and your relationship with God. After all, God is the ultimate provider, and we need to be good stewards of what He has entrusted to us.

This isn't just a pipe dream or a vague wish. A financial plan gives you direction, clarity, and purpose. It's the roadmap that takes your vision and turns it into reality. Proverbs 21:5 says, *"The plans of the diligent lead to profit as surely as haste leads to poverty."* This means that you need a plan, and that plan needs to be rooted in diligence, prayer, and purpose.

Let's dive into how you can go from having a vision of wealth to making it a reality.

Step 1: Start with Prayer and Vision

Before you even begin crafting a financial plan, it's important to set aside time for prayer. Ask God for wisdom, guidance, and clarity. Remember, Proverbs 3:5-6 says, *"Trust in the Lord with all your heart and lean not on your own understanding; in all your ways submit to him, and he will make your paths straight."* This is the foundation of everything. You're not making a financial plan on your own—you're doing it with God's direction.

Once you've prayed and asked for God's guidance, take some time to write down your vision. Where do you see yourself financially in one year, five years, and even ten years? What does prosperity look like for you? Is it being debt-free? Owning a home? Starting a business? Giving more generously to others? It's essential to write down your vision because the Bible reminds us in Habakkuk 2:2, *"Write the vision and make it plain on tablets, that he may run who reads it."*

Your vision doesn't have to be perfect right now. Just start with what God places on your heart. Keep refining it as you move forward, but make sure you have a starting point. The clearer your vision, the more focused your efforts will be.

Step 2: Break Down the Vision into Goals

Once you have your vision, it's time to break it down into short-term and long-term goals. Goals are the stepping stones that will lead you toward your vision. Proverbs 16:3 says, *"Commit to the Lord whatever you do, and he will establish your plans."* By setting goals, you're committing your financial journey to God.

Short-term goals (3 to 12 months): These are the smaller, more immediate objectives that will help you make progress toward your vision. For example, maybe your short-term goal is to pay off a credit card or save $500 in an emergency fund. Whatever it is, make sure the goal is measurable and realistic. You need something concrete to work toward.

Long-term goals (1 year to 5 years or more): These are the big-picture goals that take time and intentional effort to achieve. Maybe your long-term goal is to own a house, start a business, or achieve financial independence. Whatever your long-term goal is, break it down into smaller, more manageable chunks that you can achieve over time.

Remember, in order to make your goals work, they need to be SMART—Specific, Measurable, Achievable, Relevant, and Time-bound. This simple framework will help you stay focused and motivated as you work toward your financial objectives.

Step 3: Create a Budget Aligned with Your Faith

Now that you have your vision and your goals, it's time to get down to the details: budgeting. A budget isn't a restrictive tool; it's a tool for freedom. When you create a budget, you're taking control of your finances and ensuring that your money is working toward your goals.

The Bible gives us a clear principle in Luke 14:28-30: *"Suppose one of you wants to build a tower. Won't you first sit down and estimate the cost to see if you have enough money to complete it? For if you lay the foundation and are not able* to finish it, everyone who sees it will ridicule you, saying, 'This person began to build and wasn't able to finish.'" A budget is how you estimate the cost of your financial goals and make sure you're able to finish what you started.

Start by tracking your income and expenses. Write down how much money you bring in each month and list all of your expenses. Don't leave anything out—include everything from rent or mortgage to groceries to entertainment. Once you have this information, you can start to identify areas where you can cut back and allocate more money toward your goals.

Step 4: Establish a Savings and Investment Plan

Once you've got a handle on budgeting, it's time to look at saving and investing. Proverbs 21:20 says, *"The wise store up choice food and olive oil, but fools gulp theirs down."* This is a direct call to save and be prepared for the future. A strong financial plan includes saving for emergencies, retirement, and investments that will help you grow your wealth.

Start by building an emergency fund. Life happens—cars break down, medical bills come up, and unexpected expenses arise. Having an emergency fund will prevent you from going into debt when the unexpected happens. Aim for at least three to six months' worth of living expenses in an easily accessible account.

Once you've got your emergency fund, it's time to look at other savings and investment opportunities. What long-term goals do you have? Do you want to retire early? Send your kids to college? Start a business? Create a financial plan that includes saving for these future goals. Consider investing in stocks, real estate, or other opportunities that align with your risk tolerance and faith principles. Proverbs 13:11 says, *"Wealth gained hastily will dwindle, but whoever gathers little by little will increase it."*

Investing wisely is about steady growth and making your money work for you, not about getting rich quickly.

STEP 5: REVIEW AND Adjust Regularly

Your financial plan isn't set in stone. Life changes, and sometimes your priorities or circumstances will shift. That's why it's important to review and adjust your plan regularly. Proverbs 15:22 says, *"Plans fail for lack of counsel, but with many advisers they succeed."* Make sure to check in with your plan every few months to ensure that you're still on track. Seek counsel from trusted financial advisers, mentors, or a community of believers who can help you refine your plan and keep you accountable.

Faith in Action:

- **Regularly Assess Your Progress**: Schedule time each month to review your financial plan. Are you on track with your goals? Do you need to adjust your budget, savings, or investments?

- **Seek Wise Counsel**: Find someone you trust—whether a mentor, financial advisor, or a community group—to guide you as you grow your wealth. Don't try to do it alone.

Reflection Questions

- What is your financial vision for the next 1-3 years? What short-term and long-term goals can you set to get there?

- How can you make your financial decisions align more closely with your faith and biblical principles?

- Are there areas in your current budget where you can cut back to increase savings or give more generously?

As you go through this process, keep in mind that wealth isn't just about amassing riches. It's about using the resources God has given you to fulfill His purpose for your life. A financial plan rooted in faith is one that honors God, provides for your needs, and allows you to bless others.

Aligning Your Work with God's Calling

Alright, now we're getting into the heart of it: how can your work align with your purpose and calling in life? You might be wondering, *"What does God have in store for me when it comes to work?"* Or maybe you're thinking, "How do I figure out how to use my skills and passions in a way that's profitable and honors God?"

Well, let's break it down. Work is a huge part of our lives, and as believers, it's not just about making money—it's about doing work that reflects God's calling on your life. It's about using the talents, skills, and passions He's given you to serve others, glorify Him, and create income streams that allow you to live out your purpose.

THE BIBLE TALKS ABOUT this in Colossians 3:23-24: *"Whatever you do, work heartily, as for the Lord and not for men, knowing that from the Lord you will receive the inheritance as your reward. You are serving the Lord Christ."* This means that your work, no matter what it is, should be done with a mindset of serving God, not just chasing after money or recognition. Whether you're an entrepreneur, a teacher, a nurse, or even a stay-at-home parent, God has equipped you with skills and passions that align with His plan for your life.

Let's go step by step through the process of aligning your work with God's calling.

Step 1: Identify Your Skills and Passions

The first thing we need to do is figure out what you're good at and what you're passionate about. Many people struggle with this step, thinking that they don't have any skills or that their passions won't lead to anything practical. But

I want to tell you right now, that's not true. Every single person has been given a unique set of skills and passions by God, and those can be used to create something amazing.

Think about what you love to do. What makes you feel alive? What activities or tasks do you naturally excel at? Maybe it's writing, designing, speaking, organizing, cooking, teaching, or something else. Whatever it is, write it down. Take some time to reflect on the following questions:

- What are the things that make me excited to get out of bed in the morning?
- What are the skills that people consistently compliment me on?
- When have I felt the most energized or fulfilled while working?
- What problems do I see in the world that I would love to solve?

THESE QUESTIONS WILL help you identify the things that not only bring you joy but also showcase the skills that God has uniquely gifted you with.

Take a moment and write them down. Don't rush through this process—dig deep. Your skills and passions are key to understanding how you can align your work with God's calling.

Step 2: Recognize That Work is Not Just a Job—It's a Calling

Let's shift our perspective for a second. Many people view work as something they do just to make money. But as believers, we need to recognize that work is so much more than that. Work is a calling—a chance to serve others and God through what we do. It's about doing something that adds value to people's lives and brings glory to God.

In Ephesians 4:11-12, Paul talks about how God gave different gifts to His people: *"So Christ himself gave the apostles, the prophets, the evangelists, the pastors, and teachers, to equip his people for works of service, so that the body of Christ may be built up."* You may not be called to be a pastor or an evangelist, but God has called you to use your unique gifts to serve others, whether that's in your business, job, or community.

You may be asking yourself, **"How does this apply to me if I'm not in full-time ministry?"** Well, let me tell you this: whether you're an artist, a doctor, a teacher, or even a stay-at-home parent, your work is ministry. You have a purpose, and God is calling you to use the skills He has given you for His glory.

Step 3: Explore How Your Skills Can Create Income Streams

Okay, so we've identified your skills and passions, and we've recognized that your work is a calling. Now, how do you turn these into income streams? How can you take what you're passionate about and make money from it in a way that aligns with God's plan?

Let's take some real-life examples. I'll start with myself. When I first got into business, I didn't have all the answers. But I knew that I had a gift for teaching and helping people. I loved the idea of using my knowledge to help others achieve financial freedom. So, I started creating courses and writing books. What started as a small idea grew into a business that now generates multiple streams of income.

HERE ARE A FEW OTHER examples of people who've done the same thing:
- A chef who turned their love for cooking into a catering business or cooking classes.
- A graphic designer who started offering services to clients or created and sold design templates online.
- A writer who began freelance writing or created a blog that turned into an income stream.
- An online coach who helps others improve their fitness or finances.

The key here is to look at your skills and figure out how you can use them to create value for others. This might mean starting a side hustle, offering services to others, or creating content that can be monetized. The possibilities are endless, but the key is to align your work with your passions and purpose.

Step 4: Aligning Your Work with God's Will

Now that we've explored how to identify your skills and passions and how to turn them into income, it's time to ensure that your work aligns with God's will. How do you know if what you're doing is truly aligned with God's calling?

The answer is simple: Test it against God's Word. Does your work help others? Does it reflect His love, justice, and mercy? Are you using your income to bless others and advance His Kingdom? If the answer is yes, then you're on the right path. Proverbs 16:3 says, *"Commit to the Lord whatever you do, and he will establish your plans."* When you commit your work to God, He will guide you.

Ask yourself these questions:
- How does my work serve others and glorify God?
- Am I using my income to bless others and support God's Kingdom?
- Is my work providing value, or am I just focused on getting paid?

Your work can and should be a reflection of God's heart for His people. It's about serving others, making a difference, and doing it all for His glory.

Faith in Action

- **Start with Reflection:** Take time this week to pray and reflect on your skills and passions. Ask God to show you how He has uniquely equipped you and where He is calling you to use those gifts.

- **Create an Action Plan:** Based on your reflection, write down three specific ways you can begin using your skills to serve others and create income streams. Start with one small action step you can take today.

- **Use Your Income to Bless Others**: Identify one way you can use your income to bless others. It could be giving to a ministry, helping a friend in need, or supporting a charitable cause.

Step-by-Step Guide to Implement

1. **Reflect on Your Skills and Passions:** Write down everything you're good at and love doing. Don't rush this process—really dig deep.
2. **Commit to God's Calling:** Pray and ask God to show you how your skills align with His purpose for your life.
3. **Turn Passion into Action:** Choose one skill or passion and figure out how you can turn it into an income stream. Start small and build from there.
4. **Test Your Work Against God's Word**: Check to make sure your work aligns with God's principles. Does it serve others and glorify Him?
5. **Take Action**: Start working on your business or job with a mindset of serving God and others. Keep your vision clear, and trust that God will guide your efforts.

Reflection Questions

What skills and passions has God given me, and how can I use them to serve others?

- How can I turn one of my skills into an income stream that aligns with my purpose?

- In what ways can I ensure my work reflects God's will and adds value to His Kingdom?

Remember, your work is not just about making money. It's about doing something that honors God and makes a positive impact on the world. Align your work with God's calling, and watch as He blesses your efforts.

Budgeting as a Form of Stewardship

You might be wondering why budgeting matters so much. Is it just about controlling your spending and saving for the future? Or is there something deeper? Let's get into it.

When you think about your finances, how do you approach them? Do you let them just flow, without really thinking about where your money goes? Or do you try to control it, but find that things slip through your fingers? If you've ever been in a situation where money was tight or felt like it just vanished, you know the frustration. But here's the thing—budgeting isn't just about having control over your money; it's about being a good steward of what God has entrusted to you. It's a spiritual practice. It's about faithfulness.

Let's take a deep dive into what budgeting really is and why it's such a powerful tool for living out your faith.

What Does It Mean to Be a Steward?

First, let's talk about stewardship. The Bible tells us that everything we have comes from God. Our homes, our jobs, our talents, and yes, our money, are all gifts that God has entrusted to us. We don't own these things; we are stewards of them. A steward is someone who manages or takes care of something that belongs to someone else.

Psalm 24:1 says, *"The earth is the Lord's, and everything in it, the world, and all who live in it."* This includes your money. Everything you have is a gift from God, and it's your responsibility to manage it well. The parable of the talents (Matthew 25:14-30) is a great example of this. In the parable, the master gives his servants talents (money) and expects them to use them wisely. Those who manage the money well are rewarded, and the one who buried it is punished.

This teaches us that God expects us to wisely manage the resources He has given us.

So, how does budgeting fit into this picture? Budgeting is one of the most practical ways to manage your finances in a way that honors God and aligns with His purposes.

Why Is Budgeting an Act of Faithfulness?

When you budget, you are acknowledging that the money you have doesn't belong to you—it belongs to God. Budgeting shows that you are committed to managing your finances in a way that honors Him and helps you be faithful with what He has given you.

PROVERBS 21:5 SAYS, *"The plans of the diligent lead to profit as surely as haste leads to poverty."* This verse highlights that planning is key to achieving success. When you budget, you plan for your financial future. You allocate money for your needs, your family, and your future, but you also make sure to set aside money for generosity and God's Kingdom. It's an act of faith because it requires you to trust that God will provide as you manage your resources wisely.

When you don't budget, you may find yourself in situations where you're living paycheck to paycheck or constantly feeling like you're running out of money. But when you start to manage your money with intention, you are showing God that you are serious about being a good steward of the resources He's given you.

The Power of Budgeting for Financial Freedom

Now, let's talk about why budgeting is so important for achieving financial freedom. One of the reasons many people struggle financially is that they don't have a clear plan for their money. Without a budget, you're essentially letting your money control you instead of the other way around. You're reacting to situations instead of being proactive.

But when you budget, you're putting yourself in control. You're telling your money where to go, instead of wondering where it went. A budget gives you clarity about your income, your expenses, and your goals. It helps you see where you're spending unnecessarily and where you can cut back. More importantly, it helps you focus on your priorities.

Let's break this down. When you have a clear financial plan, you can:

1. **Live within your means:** You know exactly how much you're making and how much you're spending, so you're not overspending or racking up debt.

2. **Save for the future:** You can set aside money for emergencies, retirement, or big life goals.

3. **Be generous:** A budget allows you to plan for giving. You can intentionally set aside money for charitable donations, supporting ministries, or helping others in need.

4. **Invest in your goals**: Whether it's starting a business, going back to school, or traveling the world, budgeting helps you allocate resources toward your long-term dreams.

The Bible is full of verses that remind us of the importance of managing our resources wisely. In Luke 14:28, Jesus says, *"Suppose one of you wants to build a tower. Won't you first sit down and estimate the cost to see if you have enough money to complete it?"* This verse emphasizes the importance of planning.

Without a budget, it's like building a tower without checking if you have enough resources. You might start strong, but you'll run out of money before you finish the project.

How to Get Started with Budgeting

You might be thinking, **"Okay, this sounds great, but where do I even begin?"** Don't worry—I've got you covered. Here's a step-by-step guide to help you start budgeting as an act of stewardship.

Step 1: Track Your Income and Expenses

The first step is to know exactly how much money you're bringing in and where it's going. Write down all your sources of income—salary, side hustles, investments, etc. Then, track your expenses for a month. Write down everything you spend money on: bills, groceries, entertainment, gas, even that coffee you grab every morning. You'd be surprised at how small expenses can add up over time.

Step 2: Set Your Financial Goals

Now that you know your income and expenses, it's time to set some financial goals. Where do you want to be financially in 6 months? A year? Five years? Write down your short-term and long-term goals. Do you want to get out of debt? Save for a house? Build an emergency fund? Setting goals helps you stay focused and motivated.

Step 3: Create Your Budget

Now, it's time to create your actual budget. Start by categorizing your expenses. This can include things like:

- **Necessities:** Rent/mortgage, utilities, groceries, transportation
- **Savings:** Emergency fund, retirement, investments
- **Debt repayment:** Credit card payments, loans, etc.
- **Giving:** Tithes, charitable donations, gifts
- **Wants**: Entertainment, dining out, subscriptions, etc.

Remember, the goal is to prioritize your needs and your long-term financial health. You want to make sure you're saving, giving, and paying off debt before spending on things that aren't as essential.

Step 4: Stick to Your Budget

This is the hardest part, isn't it? Once you've created a budget, the next step is to stick to it. Be diligent, as Proverbs 21:5 reminds us. Keep track of your spending throughout the month and make adjustments as needed. If you overspend in one category, cut back in another. The key is to stay committed.

STEP 5: REVIEW AND Adjust Regularly

Your financial situation will change over time, and so will your goals. That's why it's important to review your budget regularly—at least once a month. Adjust as needed. As your income increases, for example, you may want to allocate more to savings or giving.

Step-by-Step Guide to Implement

1. Track your income and expenses for the next month. Write down everything—no matter how small.

2. Set clear financial goals—think about both short-term and long-term goals. Write them down.

3. Create your budget—categorize your expenses and make sure you're prioritizing giving, saving, and debt repayment.

4. Stick to your budget—track your expenses and make adjustments when necessary. Be diligent.

5. Review and adjust regularly—check your budget once a month to make sure you're on track and make adjustments as your financial situation changes.

Reflection Questions

- Are you being a good steward of the resources God has entrusted to you?
- How can budgeting help you align your financial goals with God's Kingdom?
- What are the areas in your life where you might need to adjust your spending in order to be more faithful with your finances?

Budgeting isn't just about numbers—it's about faith. It's about trusting God with your resources and managing them in a way that honors Him. When you budget as an act of stewardship, you're showing that you are a faithful servant, ready to do God's work with everything He has given you.

Saving and Investing for the Future

When was the last time you thought about your financial future? You know, the kind of future where you're not just surviving, but thriving—living with peace of mind, knowing that you're well-prepared for whatever life throws your way? It's a future where you have enough to support your family, help others, and still live comfortably. But here's the big question: Are you saving and investing in a way that secures that future?

As we walk through this journey of faith and finance, I want you to understand that saving and investing are not just practical necessities—they're part of your responsibility as a steward of God's resources. These are tools you can use to ensure your financial future is secure while still honoring God with your wealth.

Now, let me be clear—saving and investing aren't about hoarding wealth for yourself. It's not about selfishly building your empire. No, it's about preparing for the future in a way that honors God, provides for your needs, and allows you to be generous with others.

Let's dive into why saving and investing are so important and how you can align these practices with God's purposes in your life.

The Biblical Foundation of Saving and Investing

Let's start with a few Bible verses. You may be wondering if the Bible even talks about saving and investing. The answer is yes—and quite clearly.

In Proverbs 21:20, it says, *"The wise store up choice food and olive oil, but fools gulp theirs down."* This verse is a direct reference to saving and being wise with your resources. Just as a wise person stores up food and essentials for the future, we too should be saving and planning ahead.

Another powerful verse comes from Ecclesiastes 11:2, *"Invest in seven ventures, yes, in eight; you do not know what disaster may come upon the land."* This is a clear command to diversify your investments—don't put all your eggs in one basket. God is encouraging us to take wise, calculated risks by spreading out our investments to secure our financial future.

Jesus also spoke about the importance of wisely managing money in the parable of the talents (Matthew 25:14-30). The master in the story rewards the servants who invested their talents wisely and grew them. The servant who buried his talent in the ground was punished because he didn't put his resources to work. This is a reminder that God expects us to use the resources He gives us in ways that grow and multiply.

Saving: A Step Towards Financial Security

Saving is the first step in building a secure financial future. If you don't save, you're putting yourself at risk of financial hardship. But saving isn't just about putting money in the bank—it's about preparing for the future with wisdom and intention.

I understand that sometimes it feels like there's not enough money to save, but here's the thing: Every little bit counts. Even if you can only save a small amount at first, the habit of saving is what matters most. Think of it as a seed that you're planting. Over time, it will grow and provide the foundation for your financial future.

Proverbs 13:11 says, *"Dishonest money dwindles away, but whoever gathers money little by little makes it grow."* Saving little by little can build up over time. You don't have to save thousands at once. Start with what you can, but start now. The key is consistency.

So, how do you start saving? Let me walk you through it.

How to Start Saving
Step 1: Set Up an Emergency Fund

First and foremost, you need to have an emergency fund. This is money that's set aside for unexpected expenses—things like car repairs, medical bills, or job loss. Ideally, your emergency fund should cover 3-6 months' worth of living expenses. This fund is your financial safety net.

The best way to build your emergency fund is to start small. Set a realistic goal—maybe it's $500 or $1,000 to start. Once you hit that goal, continue saving until you have 3-6 months of expenses set aside.

Step 2: Automate Your Savings

If you want to be successful at saving, you need to make it a habit. One of the best ways to do this is by automating your savings. Set up an automatic transfer from your checking account to your savings account every payday. Even if it's a small amount, automating your savings will ensure that you're consistently putting money away for the future.

Step 3: Cut Unnecessary Expenses

Now, let's talk about the tough part—cutting expenses. I'm not saying you should deprive yourself of everything you enjoy. But take a hard look at your spending and see where you can trim the fat. Do you need to be eating out as often? Can you cancel some subscriptions you don't use? Small changes can make a big difference in your ability to save.

Investing: Growing Your Wealth for the Future

SAVING IS IMPORTANT, but saving alone isn't enough to build wealth. You need to invest your money to help it grow over time. Investing is where you put your money into assets that have the potential to appreciate—stocks, real estate, businesses, and other ventures.

In Luke 19:13, Jesus tells a parable about a nobleman who gave his servants money to invest while he was away. The servants who wisely invested their money were rewarded, while the one who didn't invest it was rebuked. This teaches us that investing is not just a good idea—it's a biblical principle.

But let me be clear: Investing isn't about taking wild risks. It's about being strategic, informed, and wise with your money. Diversification is key—don't put all your money into one stock or one property. Spread it out to reduce risk and increase your chances of success.

How to Start Investing

Step 1: Educate Yourself

Before you start investing, you need to learn. There are many different types of investments, and you need to understand what each one entails. Do you want to invest in the stock market, or would you prefer real estate? Maybe you want to invest in starting your own business. The key is to pick something that you understand and feel confident in.

Step 2: Start Small

Just like with saving, you don't need to start big when you begin investing. Start with small amounts of money that you're comfortable with. Over time, as you learn and become more confident in your investments, you can increase your contributions.

Step 3: Diversify Your Investments

As the Bible says in Ecclesiastes 11:2, *"Invest in seven ventures, yes, in eight; you do not know what disaster may come upon the land."* This is God's way of telling us to diversify our investments. Don't put all your money into one stock, one business, or one piece of property. Spread your investments out to protect yourself against risk.

Step 4: Be Patient

Investing is a long-term game. Don't expect to see huge returns overnight. As Proverbs 13:11 says, *"Whoever gathers money little by little makes it grow."* The key to successful investing is patience and consistency. Over time, your investments will grow if you continue to put money into them and let them compound.

Step-by-Step Guide to Implement

1. **Set up your emergency fund:** Aim for 3-6 months of living expenses, and save little by little until you reach your goal.

2. **Automate your savings**: Set up an automatic transfer from your checking account to your savings account every payday.

3. **Learn about investing**: Educate yourself on different investment options, and decide which one is best for you.

4. **Start small with investments**: Begin with small amounts that you're comfortable with. Focus on long-term growth.

5. **Diversify your investments**: Spread your money across different types of investments to reduce risk.

6. **Be patient and consistent**: Wealth-building takes time. Keep investing, and be patient as your wealth grows.

REFLECTION QUESTIONS

- Are you currently saving for your future? If not, what steps can you take today to start?
- What are your financial goals for the next 5, 10, or 20 years?
- How can you ensure that your investments align with God's purposes in your life?
- Are you taking wise, calculated risks when it comes to your investments, or are you playing it too safe?

Saving and investing aren't just financial decisions—they're spiritual decisions. By saving and investing wisely, you're securing your future and honoring God with the resources He has entrusted to you. You're being a faithful steward, ensuring that you can provide for your needs, help others, and be generous in the work of God's Kingdom. So, take action today. Start saving, start investing, and watch how God blesses your efforts as you faithfully manage what He has given you.

Avoiding Debt and Practicing Generosity

Debt. It's a word that can make anyone's stomach drop. It's that constant weight that follows you around, an invisible burden that restricts your financial freedom. You know the feeling. The bills piling up, the credit card statements arriving with interest rates that just keep climbing. It's exhausting, right?

But here's the good news: God has a better way. You don't have to live a life constantly strapped by debt, unable to truly live out the freedom He intends for you. In fact, God has called us to something better, something that honors Him and reflects His character—living debt-free and practicing generosity.

THE IMPORTANCE OF LIVING Debt-Free

The Bible speaks clearly about debt and its dangers. Proverbs 22:7 says, *"The rich rule over the poor, and the borrower is slave to the lender."* Debt is a form of slavery. It keeps you tied to obligations, chained to payments, and stressed about what's coming next. When you live in debt, it affects not just your finances but your emotional well-being and your ability to fulfill the purpose God has for your life.

Now, I get it. Debt is sometimes unavoidable. You may have student loans, a mortgage, or other necessary debts. But the key is avoiding unnecessary debt and working towards getting rid of any existing debt. God doesn't want us to be slaves to debt, He wants us to be free.

Romans 13:8 tells us, *"Let no debt remain outstanding, except the continuing debt to love one another."* This verse paints a beautiful picture: we are meant to owe only one thing—love. Everything else? We should aim to pay off and stay clear of. Debt, especially consumer debt, is a heavy weight that prevents us from fully walking in freedom.

How Debt Impacts Your Life

Living in debt robs you of peace. When you're tied to monthly payments and interest rates, it's hard to focus on what really matters. You're distracted. Your energy is drained, and your resources are depleted. Debt also affects your ability to be generous, to help others, and to live out the calling God has on your life.

Think about it—when you're living paycheck to paycheck, it's hard to think beyond your own immediate needs. But God wants you to be able to bless others, to use your resources for His Kingdom, and to be free from the stress of debt so you can serve Him wholeheartedly.

In Proverbs 21:5, we read, *"The plans of the diligent lead to profit as surely as haste leads to poverty."* The key here is diligence. Diligence in avoiding debt, diligence in saving, and diligence in living below your means. Being diligent with your finances allows you to avoid unnecessary debt and position yourself to be generous.

Breaking Free from Debt: A Step-by-Step Guide

Here's the good news—getting out of debt is not only possible, but it's also something God desires for you. It takes intentionality, discipline, and faith, but it's worth it. And the sooner you start, the sooner you can experience the freedom that comes with being debt-free.

Step 1: Acknowledge the Debt

The first step in breaking free from debt is acknowledging it. I know, facing your debt can feel overwhelming, but you have to take a hard look at your finances and face the reality of what you owe. Make a list of all your debts—credit cards, student loans, mortgages, car loans, and any other liabilities.

Psalm 32:5 says, *"Then I acknowledged my sin to you and did not cover up my iniquity."* Just as we must acknowledge our sin to God, we must also acknowledge our debt in order to make a change. Facing the truth is the first step to freedom.

Step 2: Create a Budget

Once you've acknowledged your debt, it's time to create a budget. A budget is a powerful tool that helps you track your spending, cut out unnecessary expenses, and create a plan to pay off your debt. Remember, Proverbs 27:23 says, *"Be sure you know the condition of your flocks, give careful attention to your herds."* This means you need to know where your money is going. By creating a budget, you're taking control of your finances.

List all your income and expenses. Identify areas where you can cut back and redirect that money towards paying off debt. Every penny counts.

Step 3: Focus on Paying Off High-Interest Debt First

Once you've created your budget, prioritize paying off your highest-interest debt first. Credit cards, payday loans, and other high-interest debts can quickly spiral out of control, so it's important to tackle them first. The goal is to reduce the amount of interest you're paying, freeing up more money to put towards other debts or savings.

In Romans 13:8, we are reminded, *"Let no debt remain outstanding..."* Take this to heart. Work hard to eliminate those debts, and soon you'll find yourself in a better financial position to save and be generous.

Step 4: Avoid New Debt

Now that you're focused on paying off your existing debt, make a vow not to incur any new debt. This is where discipline comes in. Every time you reach for your credit card, ask yourself if it's truly necessary. Can you save up for the purchase instead? Can you live without it?

Remember what Proverbs 22:26-27 says: *"Do not be one who shakes hands in pledge or puts up security for debts; if you lack the means to pay, your very bed will be snatched from under you."* Be careful about taking on debt you can't afford.

Step 5: Stay Committed to Your Debt-Free Goal

Paying off debt can take time, but stay committed. Trust that God will help you along the way. It may take years, but every step you take brings you closer to financial freedom.

Generosity: Reflecting God's Character

Now, let's talk about something that's even more exciting than getting out of debt—generosity. Generosity is a reflection of God's character. He is generous, and He calls us to be generous as well. When we live generously, we are imitating the very nature of God.

Acts 20:35 says, *"It is more blessed to give than to receive."* Generosity is a blessing—not just for the person receiving but for the one giving as well. When we give, we reflect the love and grace of God.

In 2 Corinthians 9:7, it says, *"Each of you should give what you have decided in your heart to give, not reluctantly or under compulsion, for God loves a cheerful giver."* God loves it when we give cheerfully, not out of obligation, but from a place of love and gratitude for all that He has done for us.

Generosity is not just about money—it's about giving our time, our talents, and our resources. When you're debt-free, you are in a position to give more freely and generously. Whether it's tithing at church, supporting a charity, or simply helping someone in need, generosity allows you to live out your faith in a tangible way.

Step-by-Step Guide to Implement

1. **List your debts:** Make a detailed list of all your debts, including interest rates and monthly payments.
2. **Create a budget:** Track your income and expenses. Identify areas where you can cut back.
3. **Pay off high-interest debt:** Focus on paying off the highest-interest debts first. Put all extra funds towards these debts.
4. **Avoid new debt:** Stop using credit cards for purchases. Save for big expenses instead of financing them.
5. **Live below your means:** Find ways to reduce your spending and increase your savings.
6. **Practice generosity:** Look for opportunities to give, whether it's money, time, or resources.
7. **Stay committed:** Keep your focus on becoming debt-free and living a life of generosity.

Reflection Questions

- Are you currently living with debt? What steps can you take today to begin paying it off?

- How does the burden of debt affect your peace and your ability to serve God?

- How can you become more generous with your resources, both financial and otherwise?

- Are you living according to God's principles of stewardship, or are there areas in your life where you need to realign?

Living debt-free and practicing generosity are both crucial aspects of God's plan for our finances. When we live free from the burden of debt, we can experience the peace and freedom that God intends for us. And when we live generously, we reflect His character and become a blessing to others. So, take the steps to avoid debt, get your finances in order, and become the generous person God has called you to be.

Chapter 3

Financial Literacy for Believers – Practical Skills for Wealth Building

Money Management and Wealth-Building Basics

Alright, let's get to the heart of it. We all know that money doesn't grow on trees, and there's no magic formula that guarantees wealth. But the good news is that there are basic principles of money management and wealth-building that, when followed, can lead to financial success. As a believer, it's crucial to understand that managing money wisely is part of being a good steward of the resources God has entrusted to you. This is where financial literacy comes in—not just knowing how to handle money, but understanding how it can work for you in the long run.

In this chapter, we'll dive into some of the most essential financial principles that will not only help you manage money well but also set you on the path to building wealth. These principles—like compound interest, income diversification, and financial literacy—are the building blocks of any strong financial foundation. Let's break these down and see how you can apply them in a way that honors God and creates financial freedom for you and your family.

Compound Interest – The Eighth Wonder of the World

You may have heard of compound interest before, but have you really grasped its power? Albert Einstein once called it "the eighth wonder of the world," and for good reason. Compound interest is a way for your money to grow exponentially over time. In simple terms, it means you earn interest not just on your initial investment, but also on the interest that accrues over time.

Let me give you an example. Imagine you invest $1,000 in an account that pays 5% interest per year. In the first year, you'll earn $50 in interest. But in the second year, you'll earn interest not just on the original $1,000, but on the $50 you earned the previous year. Over time, this cycle repeats, and your money grows at a much faster rate than if you were just earning interest on the initial

$1,000. This is why starting early and allowing your money to compound is so important.

In the Bible, we see the concept of stewardship repeatedly emphasized. In Matthew 25:14-30, Jesus tells the parable of the talents, where a master entrusts his servants with money to manage while he's away. The servants who wisely invest and grow the master's money are praised, while the one who buried it out of fear is rebuked. God expects us to be good stewards, and compound interest is one tool we can use to grow our wealth for His purposes.

So, let me ask you: How are you allowing your money to grow? Are you investing it in a way that takes advantage of compound interest, or are you letting it sit idle, losing value over time?

Income Diversification – Don't Put All Your Eggs in One Basket

Another key principle of wealth-building is income diversification. It's a simple yet powerful idea: don't put all your money into one source of income. In other words, don't rely on just your job, your business, or a single investment. Instead, aim to create multiple streams of income that work together to build wealth over time.

Think about it this way: if one source of income falls short or dries up, you'll have others to rely on. This is especially important in today's world, where the economy can change quickly, and job security isn't what it used to be.

Consider the example of the Apostle Paul, who worked as a tentmaker in addition to his ministry. In Acts 18:3, we read, *"And because he was a tentmaker as they were, he stayed and worked with them."* Paul didn't rely solely on donations or support from others—he had a trade that allowed him to support himself and continue his mission. While we are not all called to the same work as Paul, the principle is clear: diversifying your income sources can provide financial stability and security.

Income diversification can come in many forms. Maybe you have a full-time job, but you also invest in stocks or real estate. Perhaps you have a side business or generate passive income through royalties or affiliate marketing. Whatever the case, the key is to not rely on one single income stream. The more you can diversify, the better positioned you are to weather financial storms and take advantage of opportunities as they arise.

Ask yourself: How many income streams do you currently have? What opportunities can you explore to diversify your income and build a stronger financial foundation?

Financial Literacy – Knowledge is Power

At the core of money management and wealth-building is financial literacy. This is the understanding of how money works—how to manage it, grow it, and make it work for you. It's not about getting rich quick; it's about being educated and strategic with your finances. Unfortunately, many people are never taught the basics of financial literacy, and as a result, they struggle with debt, lack of savings, and missed opportunities.

Proverbs 4:7 says, *"The beginning of wisdom is this: Get wisdom. Though it cost all you have, get understanding."* The Bible teaches us that wisdom and understanding are invaluable, and this extends to our finances as well. The more you learn about money—how to budget, save, invest, and avoid debt—the more control you will have over your financial future.

Financial literacy isn't just about knowing how to balance a checkbook (though that's important too). It's about understanding concepts like budgeting, saving, investing, taxes, and debt management. It's about learning how to make smart decisions that will help you build wealth over time. This kind of knowledge allows you to make informed decisions that lead to greater financial security and freedom.

In practical terms, financial literacy means taking the time to read books, listen to podcasts, or watch videos on personal finance. It means seeking out a mentor or financial advisor who can help you navigate your finances. It also means taking responsibility for your own financial education, even if you didn't learn it in school.

How well do you understand your finances? Are you actively seeking to improve your financial knowledge and make better decisions with your money?

Faith in Action

Now that we've covered the basics of money management and wealth-building, it's time to put what you've learned into action. Remember, knowledge is only useful when it's applied. Here are some steps you can take today to begin managing your money better and building wealth for the future:

-**Start saving and investing:** If you haven't already, set up a savings account and start contributing regularly. Even if it's just a small amount at first, the important thing is to get into the habit of saving. Then, look into investing in a retirement account or other investment vehicles that allow your money to grow over time.

-**Track your spending**: One of the most important aspects of managing money is knowing where it's going. Use a budgeting app or a simple spreadsheet to track your income and expenses. This will help you identify areas where you can cut back and redirect that money toward savings and investments.

- **Diversify your income:** If you rely solely on a paycheck, look for ways to diversify your income. This could mean starting a side business, investing in real estate, or exploring other passive income opportunities like stocks or affiliate marketing.

-**Educate yourself:** Take time to improve your financial literacy. Read books, watch videos, and seek advice from experts who can help you understand money management and wealth-building strategies. The more you learn, the better equipped you'll be to make wise financial decisions.

Step-by-Step Guide to Implement

1. **Assess Your Current Financial Situation**: Take a good look at your finances—income, expenses, savings, and investments. Write down where you stand today.

2. **Set Financial Goals:** Define what financial success looks like for you. Is it getting out of debt? Building an emergency fund? Saving for retirement? Be clear on your goals so you can work toward them with purpose.

3. **Start Budgeting**: Create a simple budget to track your income and expenses. Identify areas where you can cut back and start saving or investing more.

4. **Open a Savings and Investment Account**: If you don't already have one, open a savings or investment account. Start small and make regular contributions.

5. **Learn and Grow:** Commit to learning more about money management and wealth-building. Read a book, listen to a podcast, or take a course on personal finance.

6. **Diversify Your Income:** Look for ways to generate additional income streams. Whether it's through a side business or investment, find opportunities to increase your cash flow.

Reflection Questions

- How well do you understand the concept of compound interest? Are you allowing your money to grow through investments that take advantage of it?

- Have you diversified your income streams? What are some ways you can add new sources of income to your financial plan?

- How financially literate do you consider yourself to be? What steps are you taking to improve your financial education?

- Are you actively managing your money, or are you letting it manage you?

Wealth-building isn't about getting rich quick or hoping for a miracle. It's about understanding and applying simple, timeless principles like compound interest, income diversification, and financial literacy. When you align your financial practices with God's wisdom, you'll find that He can bless your efforts and help you build wealth that lasts.

Entrepreneurship and Creating Multiple Streams of Income

The world is changing, and the old idea of relying on a single source of income—a single job or paycheck—isn't enough anymore. Whether you're working for someone else or building your own business, there's one truth that can't be ignored: **Entrepreneurship is key to building wealth**. The key to true financial freedom is having multiple streams of income that work for you. And trust me, this doesn't just mean having a full-time job and a side hustle; it's about building a system of income sources that, when combined, give you stability, flexibility, and growth.

Let's talk about **how entrepreneurship can help you create multiple streams of income,** and how you can use side businesses and freelance work to build wealth. I'll break it down, step by step, and show you how you can start working toward that freedom now, no matter where you are.

Entrepreneurship – Not Just for the "Lucky" Few

First off, you need to understand that **entrepreneurship isn't reserved for a select few.** It's not just for the wealthy, or for those with fancy degrees or a great business plan. Anyone can become an entrepreneur. You don't need a lot of money to get started. You don't need to have some groundbreaking new idea. You don't even need to quit your job right away.

Entrepreneurship is about *seeing opportunities and turning them into income-generating ventures*. It's about using your skills, your knowledge, and your creativity to solve problems and meet needs. God has given you talents, and it's time to use them. In Matthew 25:14-30, the Parable of the Talents tells us that when we use our resources wisely, we are rewarded. If you're sitting on your talents, waiting for the "perfect" time or idea, you're missing the point. Start where you are, with what you have.

The reality is, no one can depend solely on a salary to become wealthy. **Entrepreneurship opens up the doors to passive income**—money that keeps coming in without you having to actively work for it every hour of the day. **Multiple income streams are the key** to financial growth, and entrepreneurship is your best tool to create them.

Now, you might be asking, "Where do I start?" Let's break it down.

Side Businesses – Small Starts, Big Potential

Side businesses are the easiest way to get started as an entrepreneur, and you don't need a huge upfront investment to make them work. **A side business is something you can start alongside your regular job or responsibilities** to generate extra income. The beauty of side businesses is that they can grow at your pace, and once they gain momentum, they can turn into full-time ventures.

Here are a few ideas for side businesses that are simple, effective, and in demand right now:

1. **Freelancing:** If you have a skill, such as writing, graphic design, web development, or even social media management, freelancing is an excellent way to start earning extra income. You can sign up on platforms like Upwork, Fiverr, or Freelancer, and start offering your services to clients worldwide. This is low-cost to start and offers flexibility, meaning you can scale up or down as needed.

2. **Online Coaching**: Do you have expertise in a certain area? Whether it's fitness, personal development, business, or even cooking, you can offer online coaching services. Use platforms like Zoom or Skype to conduct sessions, and leverage social media to build your brand and attract clients. You'd be surprised how many people are willing to pay for advice, especially if you can show them results.

3. **Affiliate Marketing**: If you're into marketing or just love recommending products, affiliate marketing is a great way to earn money by promoting products you love. Platforms like Amazon Associates or ClickBank make it easy for you to earn commissions on sales made through your affiliate links. The key is to build trust with your audience and consistently recommend quality products.

4. **E-commerce**: With platforms like Etsy, eBay, or even Amazon, it's easier than ever to start selling products online. Whether it's handmade goods, vintage items, or something else, there's a market for nearly anything. E-commerce businesses can start small and scale quickly, especially if you can find a unique niche or product.

5. **Real Estate Investing**: While this might require more upfront capital, **real estate investing is one of the most powerful ways to build wealth**. Whether you're buying properties to rent or flipping houses, real estate has long been a staple of wealth-building. If you don't have the capital to start, consider partnering with others, using platforms like Fundrise or REITs (Real Estate Investment Trusts).

6. **Content Creation:** Do you have a passion for making videos, writing, or photography? Content creation—whether for YouTube, a blog, or Instagram—can be a fantastic source of income. With the rise of monetization programs like YouTube Partner Program, Patreon, and brand sponsorships, there are plenty of ways to earn money by doing something you enjoy.

The key with side businesses is **to start small and scale over time.** You don't need to leave your job or take on huge risks right away. Start by dedicating a few hours a week to your side business, and as it grows, you can adjust your time and efforts accordingly. Remember, it's about **building a foundation** that can support you financially in the future.

Freelance Work – Using Your Skills for Freedom

In today's world, freelancing has become a significant opportunity for anyone with a skill and the desire to create their own income. Whether it's writing, web design, consulting, or even virtual assistance, freelancing allows you to be your own boss while earning money on the side.

The Bible speaks about the importance of using your skills wisely, in Matthew 25:14-30, where each servant is given talents according to their ability. God expects us to multiply those talents, and freelancing is one way to use them effectively. Freelancing can be done on your schedule, and the beauty is that **you can leverage multiple platforms** to get started.

Here are a few steps to get into freelancing:

1. **Assess Your Skills:** Start by making a list of your skills. What are you good at? What do you enjoy doing? This will help you decide what kind of freelance work you can offer.

2. **Create a Portfolio:** Clients want to see examples of your work before they hire you. Build a simple portfolio showcasing your best work. If you're just starting, consider doing some pro-bono work to build your portfolio.

3. **Join Freelance Platforms**: Websites like Upwork, Fiverr, and Freelancer are great platforms to find clients looking for your services. These platforms help you build credibility and gain experience, even if you're just starting out.

4. **Set Your Rates and Time**: One of the benefits of freelancing is that you can set your own rates. However, be sure to research industry standards so you don't undervalue your services. Also, decide how much time you want to dedicate to freelancing based on your schedule.

5. **Network and Grow**: Word of mouth is still one of the most powerful marketing tools. As you gain experience and build relationships with clients, ask for referrals. This can lead to more business down the line.

Creating Multiple Streams of Income – The Secret to Financial Freedom

The magic happens when you **combine multiple streams of income**. Side businesses and freelance work are just the beginning. As you grow your income, think about how you can build additional streams—whether it's through investments, creating a digital product, or starting an online course.

Remember, *the goal is not to overwhelm yourself.* Start with one or two income streams and gradually build over time. The more you diversify your sources of income, the more financial freedom you'll have. This means **you won't be solely dependent on your 9-to-5 job** to cover all your expenses. Instead, you'll have income coming in from multiple places, giving you more financial security.

Proverbs 13:11 reminds us, *"Wealth gained hastily will dwindle, but whoever gathers little by little will increase it."* The same principle applies here—**slow and steady wins the race**. Don't rush into everything at once. Focus on one stream at a time, and build your wealth slowly but surely.

Faith in Action

1. **Pick Your First Side Business:** Choose one of the side business ideas we discussed, and commit to spending a few hours a week working on it. Start small, and be consistent.

2. **Set Clear Financial Goals:** What do you want to achieve with your side business? Do you want to earn $500 a month, or do you want to replace your full-time income? Set measurable, realistic goals for your business.

3. **Create a Plan:** Write out a step-by-step plan for your business, including how much time you'll dedicate, how you'll attract clients or customers, and how you'll manage your finances.

4. **Leverage Your Network**: Tell your friends and family about your new venture. You'd be surprised how many opportunities can come from word of mouth.

5. **Invest in Learning**: Keep learning and improving your skills. The more you grow, the more valuable you become to your clients or customers.

Step-by-Step Guide to Implement

1. Assess Your Skills and Interests: Think about your passions and talents. What can you do that people would pay for?

2. Choose Your First Income Stream: Start small with something manageable—freelance writing, graphic design, or selling a product.

3. Set Time Commitments: Dedicate a set amount of time each week to your side business.

4. Create a Budget and Set Financial Goals: Understand how much money you need to make and track your progress.

5. Grow and Scale: As you gain experience, expand your efforts to include more streams of income.

ARE YOU READY TO STEP out of your comfort zone and start building multiple streams of income? What's holding you back?

Planning for Retirement and Legacy Building

Alright, my friend, let's talk about something that often gets overlooked in the hustle of everyday life—**long-term financial planning**. Specifically, we're diving into two of the most crucial aspects of financial freedom: **retirement planning** and **legacy building**. These aren't just things that the rich think about; they're things that **everyone** should be thinking about, no matter where you're at in life.

You see, the truth is this: **We don't work forever**, and neither should our wealth. A well-thought-out plan for retirement ensures that you'll have the freedom to live comfortably when you can't (or don't want to) work anymore. But beyond retirement, there's a much bigger question to consider: **What will you leave behind?** This is where legacy building comes into play.

Building a legacy isn't just about leaving money behind for your family (though that's part of it). It's about creating a lasting impact—on your family, on your church, and on your community. **It's about passing on more than just financial wealth**; it's about passing on wisdom, values, faith, and opportunities. In this subchapter, we'll walk through why planning for retirement is important, and how you can **build a legacy** that will continue to benefit your loved ones and others for generations.

Why Plan for Retirement?

Listen, retirement doesn't just happen. It doesn't come as a reward after years of work—it comes because you plan for it. Too many people ignore the reality of **retirement planning** until they're too old or too financially strained to do anything about it. But here's the thing: The earlier you start, the better.

Planning for retirement isn't just about stashing away money; it's about setting up a system that will continue to provide for you and your loved ones when you're no longer working. Proverbs 21:5 says, *"The plans of the diligent lead to profit as surely as haste leads to poverty."*

Retirement planning is a marathon, not a sprint. But the beautiful part is that it doesn't have to be complicated. You don't need to be rich to start planning for the future. The key is consistency, and starting now—no matter how small the steps are.

The Power of Compounding: Let's Talk Numbers

Let me tell you about one of the most powerful financial principles: **compound interest**. This is the magic that makes retirement planning work. Simply put, compound interest is the process where your money earns interest on the original amount, and then that interest earns more interest, and so on. It's like planting a seed today and watching it grow into a tree tomorrow.

Here's the kicker: The earlier you start, the more time your money has to grow. If you start saving for retirement in your twenties, your investments will have decades to compound. But if you wait until your forties or fifties, you miss out on those extra years of growth.

Consider this: If you invested $100 per month from age 25 to 65, and earned an average return of 7% per year, you would end up with $235,000. But if you waited just 10 years and started at age 35, you would have only $140,000 at the same rate of return. That's a $95,000 difference simply because you waited. Time is the secret ingredient to building wealth for retirement.

Retirement Strategies

There are several strategies you can use to start building your retirement fund. It doesn't matter if you're working for someone or running your own business—there's a plan for you.

1. **Employer-Sponsored Retirement Plans**: If you're employed, the first place to start is any retirement plan your employer offers, like a 401(k). This is the easiest way to begin saving because often, employers will match your contributions up to a certain percentage. If your employer offers this, it's essentially free money, so take advantage of it.

2. **Individual Retirement Accounts (IRA)**: Whether or not your employer offers a plan, **IRAs** are another great way to save for retirement. There are traditional IRAs and Roth IRAs, and both offer tax advantages. With a **Roth IRA,** for instance, you contribute money that's already taxed, but your withdrawals are tax-free after you retire. This can be a great option if you think your taxes will be higher in retirement than they are now.

3. **Investments:** If you want to build wealth for retirement beyond just savings accounts, **investing** is a powerful tool. Stocks, bonds, mutual funds, and real estate all have the potential to offer better returns over the long term than traditional savings accounts.

4. **Diversifying Your Assets**: It's important to not just save money, but to have your money working for you in multiple places. You can diversify by investing in stocks, bonds, real estate, or even starting your own business. This way, you spread out your risks, and you give yourself multiple opportunities for growth.

Creating a Legacy: More Than Money

So, now that we've covered retirement, let's talk about legacy. *What do you want to be remembered for?* What will your children, your grandchildren, and even your community say about you when you're gone?

Building a legacy goes far beyond **wealth**. Sure, leaving a financial inheritance is great, but a legacy is much more profound than just the amount of money you leave behind. It's about passing on values, wisdom, opportunities, and faith to those who come after you. Your legacy is your impact on the world.

As believers, our legacy should reflect the values of God's kingdom. We are stewards of what God has given us, and it's our responsibility to manage not just our money, but also the lives and resources He's entrusted to us.

Let's look at the example of David in the Bible. In 1 Chronicles 28:9, David charges his son Solomon to follow God with his whole heart. He doesn't just leave Solomon with wealth; he leaves him with wisdom, encouragement, and a plan for building the temple. That's the kind of legacy we should aim to leave behind—a legacy rooted in **faith** and **purpose**.

Your legacy might include:

-Creating a foundation or scholarship fund for those in need in your community or church.

-Mentoring and investing in the younger generation to ensure they're prepared for life and the world ahead.

- Sharing your faith in a way that continues to inspire others even after you're gone.

-Providing for your family so they can continue building on the foundation you set.

The truth is, **a legacy doesn't happen by accident.** It takes intention and planning. You need to think about your long-term goals and your values, and then work backward to see how you can build that legacy today. Whether it's through charity, mentorship, or financial planning, your legacy is about building something that outlives you.

Faith in Action: Planning for Your Future

Now that we've talked about retirement and legacy building, it's time to take action. Here's how you can start building your own retirement plan and legacy today:

Step-by-Step Guide to Implement

1. **Start with a Vision:** What do you want your retirement to look like? Do you want to travel? Do you want to serve others more? Take some time to write down your vision for the future.

2. **Create a Retirement Plan**: Begin by contributing to your employer's retirement plan or starting your own IRA. If you're self-employed, consider investing in a **SEP IRA** or **Solo 401(k).** Make saving a regular habit.

3. **Invest Wisely:** Research investment options that align with your goals. Learn about stocks, bonds, mutual funds, and real estate. Begin to diversify your assets for long-term growth.

4. **Think About Your Legacy:** What do you want to leave behind? Start planning for a legacy that includes both financial wealth and the transfer of wisdom, faith, and values to those who come after you.

5. **Give Back to Your Community**: Whether it's through your time, talents, or financial support, think about how you can make a difference in the lives of others. Giving is a key part of building a legacy that reflects God's love.

6. **Start Early:** The earlier you start planning, the more time you'll have to build a meaningful legacy. Don't wait for "the perfect time." The time to act is now.

Reflection Question

What kind of legacy do you want to leave behind?

Are you planning for the future of your family, church, and community?

What actions can you take today to ensure that your legacy is one of impact, faith, and love?

Chapter 4

The Hard Truth About Faith and Finances – Wisdom, Work, and Wealth

Let's address the elephant in the room—the myths, misconceptions, and sometimes outright lies that keep believers broke, frustrated, and confused about why their financial situations never improve despite their deep faith and endless devotion to spiritual practices like tithing, offering, fasting, and prayers.

If you're ready to hear the unfiltered truth, buckle up. It's time to dismantle the harmful beliefs that have held many back and reveal what God truly wants for your financial life.

The Role of Tithing and Offering

Tithing and giving offerings are biblical principles. They are acts of obedience and worship, designed to honor God and support the work of His Kingdom. Malachi 3:10 speaks of the blessings that come when we tithe faithfully, saying:

> *"Bring the whole tithe into the storehouse, that there may be food in my house. Test me in this,"* says the Lord Almighty, *"and see if I will not throw open the floodgates of heaven and pour out so much blessing that there will not be room enough to store it."*

But here's the hard truth: **Tithing and offering alone will not guarantee financial freedom.**

Why? Because they are part of a bigger picture, not the whole solution.

SOME PEOPLE TITHE FAITHFULLY yet live paycheck to paycheck. Others give generously every Sunday but can't seem to break free from the chains of debt. Meanwhile, there are individuals who never tithe yet succeed financially and even impact others' lives in genuine, transformative ways. What's going on?

The truth is that tithing, offering, fasting, and prayer are spiritual principles, but financial freedom requires **practical principles** too. God has set up a world where effort, discipline, and wisdom are rewarded.

Why Faithful Tithers Sometimes Struggle Financially

1. Lack of Financial Discipline

Tithing and giving are not substitutes for budgeting, saving, or investing. You can tithe faithfully but still waste money on unnecessary expenses, poor financial decisions, or get-rich-quick schemes. Financial stewardship requires discipline.

2. Misinterpretation of Scriptures

Some people treat tithing as a transactional arrangement with God. They think, *"If I tithe, God owes me a financial breakthrough."* But tithing is not a lottery ticket. It is an act of faith, not a shortcut to riches.

---

3. Ignoring Hard Work and Wisdom

Proverbs 14:23 reminds us:

> *"All hard work brings a profit, but mere talk leads only to poverty."*

You cannot tithe your way to wealth without putting in the effort and using the wisdom God has given you. It's like planting a seed but refusing to water it, expecting it to grow on its own.

4. Blind Giving and Manipulation

Let's talk about those who empty their entire wallets in church under the guise of "covenants" or "spiritual directions," only to go home broke. This is not faith; it is foolishness. God does not require you to make reckless decisions in the name of worship. Luke 14:28 says:

> *"Suppose one of you wants to build a tower. Won't you first sit down and estimate the cost to see if you have enough money to complete it?"*

Faith and wisdom go hand in hand. God honors intentionality, not recklessness.

Why Non-Tithers Sometimes Succeed Financially

It's uncomfortable to admit, but many non-believers or non-tithers achieve financial success and even contribute positively to society. How? Because they follow principles that work, regardless of faith:

-Hard Work: They put in the effort, sometimes more than believers who rely solely on prayer.

- Strategic Planning: They budget, save, and invest wisely.

- Discipline: They avoid frivolous spending and focus on long-term goals.

God's principles for wealth creation, like sowing and reaping, apply universally. If you work diligently, steward your resources wisely, and remain disciplined, the results will follow, regardless of whether you tithe.

Balancing Spiritual and Practical Principles

Let me be clear: This is not an argument against tithing, offering, or spiritual disciplines. These practices honor God and align your heart with His Kingdom. But they must be combined with practical action. Faith without works is dead (James 2:26).

If you tithe, also budget. If you give offerings, also invest. If you pray for a financial breakthrough, also work hard and develop marketable skills. God blesses the work of your hands—not the dreams in your mind that you never act on.

Your Financial Success Matters to God

For too long, some have equated poverty with humility or holiness. But there is nothing holy about being unable to feed your family or support your church. **Your success is as important to God as your salvation.**

John 10:10 says:

> *"I have come that they may have life, and have it to the full."*

A full life includes spiritual abundance, yes, but also the ability to live without constant financial stress, to give generously, and to leave a legacy for your family and community.

PRACTICAL STEPS TO Financial Freedom

If you're ready to take charge of your financial life, here are actionable steps to get started:

1. Tithe with Purpose

Tithing is about putting God first. Do it with a cheerful heart, but don't neglect the other principles of financial management.

2. Create a Budget

Track your income and expenses. Know where your money is going and allocate it wisely.

3. Save and Invest

Set aside a portion of your income for emergencies and future growth. Learn about investment opportunities and make your money work for you.

4. Develop Marketable Skills

Whether it's freelancing, entrepreneurship, or learning a trade, acquire skills that can increase your income.

5. Avoid Debt

Live within your means and resist the temptation to borrow for unnecessary expenses.

6. Give Intentionally

Be generous, but also wise. Don't give out of guilt or manipulation. Pray for discernment and give where it will have the most impact.

7. Trust God and Work Hard

Pray for guidance, but also take action. God blesses those who step out in faith and work diligently.

STOP USING SCRIPTURE to Justify Ignorance

It's time to stop misusing scripture to justify poor financial decisions. Don't spiritualize laziness, recklessness, or a lack of planning. God has given you wisdom—use it!

Proverbs 4:7 reminds us:

> *"The beginning of wisdom is this: Get wisdom. Though it cost all you have, get understanding."*

Wisdom is not only for spiritual matters but also for practical living, including your finances.

God wants you to succeed—not just spiritually but also financially. Your financial freedom is not a selfish desire; it is part of God's plan for you to live a life of abundance and generosity. Use your resources wisely, honor God with your wealth, and build a legacy that inspires others.

Faith in Action

- **Review Your Finances**: Write down your income, expenses, and giving habits. Identify areas for improvement.
- **Set Financial Goals**: Decide on short-term and long-term goals, such as paying off debt or saving for an investment.
- **Commit to Growth**: Pray for wisdom and take actionable steps to improve your financial knowledge and skills.

Reflection Questions

1. Are you relying solely on spiritual practices for financial breakthrough, or are you also taking practical steps?

2. How can you balance faith and wisdom in your financial decisions?

3. Are you using your wealth to honor God and help others, or are you stuck in a cycle of lack and frustration?

It's time to step out of the shadows of financial struggle and into the light of God's abundance. The choice is yours. Will you take it?

Faith Without Action Leads to Frustration

Let's face it—there's a hard truth many churches are too polite, or perhaps too scared, to say outright. **You cannot pray your way out of poverty without action.** You cannot fast your way to financial freedom without strategy. And no, you cannot tithe or give offerings enough to erase poor financial habits or an unwillingness to work hard.

It's time we confront the realities that too many believers avoid. If we continue to lean solely on spiritual practices while ignoring the practical, we are not only setting ourselves up for failure—we are misrepresenting God's principles for success.

WHY PRAYERS ALONE WON'T Make You Rich

Prayer is powerful. It connects us to God, aligns our hearts with His will, and brings peace and clarity. But here's the truth: Prayer without action leads to frustration.

James 2:17 couldn't be clearer:

> *"In the same way, faith by itself, if it is not accompanied by action, is dead."*

Praying for financial breakthrough while sitting idle is like asking God to bless an empty field. No seed, no rain, no labor—just expectations. God can only bless what you bring to Him. If you refuse to work, learn, or grow, your prayers become empty noise.

The Misuse of Tithing and Offering

Many believers treat tithing and offerings like spiritual investments with guaranteed returns. They expect a hundredfold harvest for every dollar they give, but life doesn't work that way. Yes, tithing is important. Yes, God blesses cheerful givers. But let me ask you this:

- What happens when you tithe but remain in financial ignorance?

- How does God bless someone who refuses to manage their resources wisely?

- Why do so many tithe faithfully yet struggle to pay their bills?

The answer is simple: God is not a magician. He honors principles, not empty rituals. Proverbs 13:11 says:

> *"Dishonest money dwindles away, but whoever gathers money little by little makes it grow."*

If you tithe but squander the rest of your income, you're not honoring God—you're testing Him.

The Danger of Religious Manipulation

Let's get even more uncomfortable. Too many Christians have been deceived by manipulation disguised as faith. Some preachers urge congregants to empty their wallets in the name of "sowing a seed" or "sealing a covenant." Others sell the idea that financial success requires extravagant acts of giving.

This is not faith—it's exploitation. God does not need your last dime to bless you. He doesn't require you to give out of guilt or desperation. 2 Corinthians 9:7 makes it clear:

> *"Each of you should give what you have decided in your heart to give, not reluctantly or under compulsion, for God loves a cheerful giver."*

Blindly giving away your rent money or grocery budget isn't faith—it's foolishness. God gave you wisdom for a reason.

The Success of Non-Believers

Now let's address an uncomfortable question: Why do some non-believers succeed financially without tithing, fasting, or even praying?

The answer is simple: They follow principles that work.

- They budget their income.
- They invest in assets.
- They work hard and improve their skills.

God's principles for financial success, such as diligence and stewardship, are universal. Whether you're a believer or not, these principles apply. Matthew 5:45 reminds us:

> *"He causes his sun to rise on the evil and the good, and sends rain on the righteous and the unrighteous."*

God's View on Financial Success

Let's be clear: God wants you to succeed financially. Your financial success is not selfish; it is a tool to impact lives, advance His Kingdom, and provide for your family.

Deuteronomy 8:18 states:

> *"But remember the Lord your God, for it is he who gives you the ability to produce wealth, and so confirms his covenant, which he swore to your ancestors, as it is today."*

Wealth is not the enemy—greed is. Money is not the problem—it's how you manage it.

Breaking the Cycle of Financial Struggle

If you've been stuck in a cycle of financial struggle despite your faithfulness in tithing, offering, fasting, and prayer, it's time to face reality: You need to change your approach.

1. Educate Yourself

Learn about budgeting, saving, investing, and wealth creation. Financial ignorance is one of the main reasons many believers remain broke.

2. Work Diligently

Stop waiting for a miracle job or a mysterious "destiny helper." Put your hands to work. Proverbs 10:4 says:

> *"Lazy hands make for poverty, but diligent hands bring wealth."*

3. Invest Wisely

Don't just save money—make it grow. Learn about investment opportunities, start a side hustle, or acquire skills that increase your earning potential.

4. Stop Spiritualizing Poor Decisions

Don't blame the devil for financial mistakes that are your responsibility. Stop using scripture to justify reckless giving or poor stewardship.

5. Balance Spiritual and Practical Principles

Pray and fast, but also budget and plan. Tithe and give, but also save and invest. Faith and wisdom are not opposites—they are partners.

The Call to Wake Up

It's time to wake up, Church. Stop romanticizing poverty as a sign of godliness or a test of faith. Stop preaching financial dependence when God has called us to be lenders, not borrowers (Deuteronomy 28:12). Stop hiding behind spiritual practices while ignoring the practical principles that lead to success.

God is not glorified by your financial struggles. He is glorified when you use the wealth He has entrusted to you to bless others, advance His Kingdom, and live a life of purpose.

Faith in Action

- Audit Your Financial Practices: Are you relying solely on spiritual disciplines for financial success? Identify areas where you need practical improvement.

- Set Practical Goals: Write down specific financial goals and create a step-by-step plan to achieve them.

- Invest in Wisdom: Take a course, read a book, or seek mentorship to improve your financial knowledge.

Reflection Questions

1. Are you balancing spiritual and practical principles in your financial life?
2. Have you been manipulated into giving recklessly instead of wisely?
3. How can you honor God with both your faith and your finances?

The hard truth may sting, but it's necessary. God has equipped you with everything you need to succeed—faith, wisdom, and the ability to work. The question is, will you use them?

Chapter 5

Leaving a Legacy – Impacting Future Generations

Teaching the Next Generation about Faith and Finances

Alright, let's get real for a moment. You and I both know that **the next generation** is going to face a whole new set of financial challenges. They'll be navigating a world that's evolving faster than ever before—technologies, markets, and even economies are shifting. And it's our job to ensure they're equipped to deal with it, not just in terms of **knowledge,** but also in terms of **values.**

But here's the thing: No matter how much you earn, or how much you accumulate, if you don't teach the next generation about faith and finances, all your hard work could be in vain. Teaching them to be good stewards of the resources God has entrusted to us is more than just teaching them how to handle money. It's about showing them how to integrate faith with finance, how to be generous, how to plan for the future, and most importantly, how to honor God with their resources.

The goal isn't just to pass on the wealth you've accumulated—it's to teach them the wisdom to manage what God gives them, whether it's a little or a lot. And let me tell you something, my friend: This is where the impact starts. You're not just teaching your children about how to balance a checkbook; you're showing them how to honor God with every dollar they handle.

Let's dive into how you can teach the next generation about faith and finances, and why it's essential to pass on this knowledge to ensure they build a solid foundation for their own future.

WHY TEACH FINANCIAL Stewardship?

There's an old saying, **"Give a man a fish, and you feed him for a day. Teach a man to fish, and you feed him for a lifetime."** This applies perfectly when it comes to teaching **the next generation** about financial stewardship. If you simply give them money or teach them about short-term fixes, you're not equipping them for life. But if you teach them the principles of financial stewardship, they'll be able to handle whatever comes their way.

In Proverbs 22:6, the Bible says, *"Train up a child in the way he should go; even when he is old he will not depart from it."* The key word here is "train." **Teaching** is one thing, but **training** is something else entirely. Training involves practice, consistency, and living out the lessons you want to pass on. It's about showing them how to live out biblical principles in a world that often offers contrary advice.

The Biblical Foundation of Financial Stewardship

Before we dive into the practical ways of teaching financial stewardship, let's first talk about the biblical foundation that should be the bedrock of everything you teach.

1. **God is the owner of everything:** Psalm 24:1 says, *"The earth is the Lord's, and everything in it, the world, and all who live in it."* We don't own anything. God owns it all. This should be the first lesson we pass on to the next generation: Everything we have is a gift from God, and we are stewards, not owners. Teaching them this helps them understand that they are responsible for handling money wisely, and it shifts their mindset from a consumer mentality to a stewardship mentality**.

2. **We're called to be generous:** Proverbs 11:25 says, *"A generous person will prosper; whoever refreshes others will be refreshed."* Generosity isn't just about giving; it's about reflecting the heart of God. By teaching them to give—whether it's to the church, to charity, or to people in need—we show them that true wealth is found in giving, not hoarding.

3. **We should be wise and avoid debt**: Proverbs 22:7 says, *"The rich rule over the poor, and the borrower is slave to the lender."* Teaching your children about avoiding unnecessary debt and using wisdom when it comes to spending is crucial. Being financially free isn't about how much you make—it's about how much you keep and how wisely you use it.

4. **Work is honorable**: Genesis 2:15 tells us that God put man in the garden to work it and take care of it. Work isn't a punishment—it's part of

God's plan for us. Teaching the next generation that work is honorable and financial growth is earned through hard work and diligence sets them up for success.

Practical Ways to Teach the Next Generation

How can you actually teach your children about finances in a way that sticks? How can you integrate faith and finances in their everyday lives? Here's a step-by-step guide:

1. **Involve Them in Your Own Financial Decisions**

One of the most effective ways to teach is by example. Let them see **how you make financial decisions**. For instance, when you're budgeting, explain why you allocate certain amounts for savings, tithing, or giving to others. Let them be part of the process, so they can understand the thought behind the decisions you make.

Ask yourself: Do they know why you tithe? Do they understand your saving goals? When they see you living out your financial decisions, it makes it more real for them.

2. **Teach Them the Basics of Budgeting and Saving**

Start teaching them the basics of budgeting as early as possible. Even if they're young, you can give them a small amount of money and show them how to divide it into categories like savings, giving, and spending. Create a fun exercise where they make a mini-budget for themselves based on their allowance or money gifts.

Let them see the principle of paying yourself first by putting money aside for the future, just as you do. You can also teach them how to set financial goals—both short-term and long-term—and how to track their progress.

3. **Teach Them the Value of Generosity**

Give your children opportunities to practice generosity. Whether it's giving part of their allowance to the church or helping someone in need, generosity is one of the best lessons you can pass on. Teach them to give with a cheerful heart (2 Corinthians 9:7), not out of obligation. Show them how their generosity blesses others and how it brings joy to their own hearts.

Ask them: How does it feel to give to others? Encourage them to reflect on the joy that comes from being generous.

4. **Use Real-Life Examples**

Another effective way to teach is through real-life examples. For instance, if you've made a big purchase or an investment, explain why you made that choice and how it fits into your **long-term plan**. Or, if you're facing a financial challenge, share how you are approaching it through **prayer, faith, and practical steps**.

5. Discuss Biblical Stories of Financial Stewardship

The Bible is full of stories that illustrate financial principles. Talk to your children about the parable of the talents (Matthew 25:14-30) and how the servants were entrusted with different amounts of money. Explain how the master expected them to be faithful with what they had been given. Teach them that God's expectations are the same for us: to wisely steward the resources He has given us.

Step-by-Step Guide to Implement

1. **Have a Family Meeting:** Sit down with your children and talk about money. Share the values of stewardship, saving, giving, and investing. Let them know that this is a lifelong lesson, not just something you talk about once and forget.

2. **Create a Budget Together**: Set up a family budget and let your kids help you categorize income and expenses. This is a great way to teach them about priorities, and it helps them understand how money is managed in a real-world context.

3. **Open a Savings Account**: If they're old enough, help them open a savings account. Encourage them to set goals and make regular deposits. Show them the value of watching their savings grow.

4. **Practice Generosity**: As a family, choose a charity or community project where you can all contribute—either through money or service. Make it a regular part of your family routine to give back.

5. **Encourage Financial Goals**: Help your children set **financial goals**, whether it's saving for something they want or planning for the future. Teach them how to track their progress and celebrate milestones.

Reflection Question

What financial lessons are you passing down to the next generation?

Are you actively teaching them the principles of stewardship, generosity, and hard work?

How are you living out your financial values in a way that they can see and emulate?

Let this be your challenge: **Start today*** by teaching the next generation the wisdom of managing finances with faith and integrity.

Using Wealth to Transform Lives and Communities

Let's cut to the chase here—money isn't just for buying things or building bigger houses. Sure, it serves a purpose in your own life, but the true power of wealth goes way beyond personal gain. When you understand the **responsibility** that comes with the wealth God has entrusted to you, you start to see that **your wealth can be a tool for transformation**, not only for yourself but for entire communities and generations to come.

You see, in 1 Timothy 6:17-19, Paul tells us, *"Command those who are rich in this present world not to be arrogant nor to put their hope in wealth, which is so uncertain, but to put their hope in God, who richly provides us with everything for our enjoyment. Command them to do good, to be rich in good deeds, and to be generous and willing to share."* God has not given us wealth to keep to ourselves or to flaunt. We are stewards, and that means we must look beyond our own needs and consider how our wealth can make an **impact** on others.

This isn't just some nice idea or "feel-good" concept. This is a biblical mandate. If you've been blessed with wealth, it's your responsibility to use it wisely and in a way that transforms lives and impacts communities for the better.

Now, let me ask you—what's the point of building wealth if it doesn't bring about positive change?

How are you going to use your resources to make a difference?

I'm going to show you how you can use your wealth to not only elevate your own life but also change the lives of those around you—and I'm not talking about just short-term fixes. I'm talking about creating lasting, generational impact.

The Biblical Call to Use Wealth for Transformation

In Proverbs 11:25, it says, *"A generous person will prosper; whoever refreshes others will be refreshed."* Generosity isn't just a nice idea—it's a principle that, when followed, can transform not just individuals but whole communities. And when you think about it, your wealth is a means to an end. It's not the end itself. Your wealth can be used to fund schools, support local businesses, provide scholarships, and, most importantly, build up the kingdom of God.

The Bible gives us several examples of how wealth can be used for good, especially for community transformation. Joseph in the Old Testament is one of the prime examples. After being sold into slavery and rising to power in Egypt, Joseph didn't hoard his wealth or live a life of excess. He used his position to store up grain during years of abundance, which helped save his family and the surrounding nations during a time of famine (Genesis 41:47-57). His wealth didn't stay with him; it became a source of provision for others, ensuring the survival of many people.

Another great example is King Solomon. Not only did Solomon use his wealth to build the temple of God (1 Kings 6), but he also invested in wisdom and knowledge. This wasn't just for his own benefit—it was for the benefit of his people. Solomon's wealth served a much greater purpose, as it helped to build a legacy of wisdom and prosperity that influenced generations after him.

So, what does that mean for you and me today? It means that your wealth is a tool, a means to serve others, support initiatives, and build long-term legacies. It's about thinking beyond your own lifetime and investing in future generations.

How Can You Use Wealth to Transform Lives?

There are a lot of ways you can begin using your wealth for good. The opportunities are endless, but let's break it down into a few key areas where your wealth can have a lasting impact.

1. Supporting Educational Initiatives

Education is one of the most powerful tools you can provide for transforming lives. Whether it's helping someone afford a college education, sponsoring a child's schooling, or funding programs that teach people valuable skills, education is a key to breaking the cycle of poverty.

You don't need to be a billionaire to make a difference. Maybe you can start small by contributing to a local school, funding scholarships for underprivileged students, or even sponsoring an after-school program. Jesus Himself was a teacher, and He valued knowledge and wisdom. Think about how you can invest in the future of someone else's life.

For instance, you could:

- Sponsor a child's education: There are many programs around the world where you can support a child's education for a relatively small amount.

- Create a scholarship fund: If you have the means, setting up a scholarship fund for underprivileged students can open doors for them that they might never have had.

-Invest in adult education: Help people acquire skills that will improve their lives, such as vocational training programs or business development courses.

The impact of these initiatives can extend for generations, and the return on that investment will last far beyond your own lifetime.

2. Funding Community Development Projects

Another powerful way to use your wealth is by funding projects that build and strengthen communities. Whether it's improving infrastructure, creating job opportunities, or helping people start small businesses, community development can create a ripple effect that helps everyone involved.

You can invest in:

- Building community centers: These spaces provide a place for people to gather, learn, and connect. It can be a resource for young people to learn skills or for families to access resources.

-Providing micro-loans for small businesses: Investing in local businesses can help create jobs and spur economic growth within the community. With a small investment, you can change lives by helping someone build their business and their future.

- Supporting healthcare initiatives: Health is wealth, as the saying goes. Investing in healthcare infrastructure, such as clinics, hospitals, or mobile health services, can drastically improve the quality of life in underserved areas.

In Acts 4:34-35, it says, *"There were no needy persons among them. From time to time those who owned land or houses sold them, brought the money from the sales, and put it at the apostles' feet, and it was distributed to anyone who had need."* This example of community care shows us that wealth can be used to meet people's needs—both physical and spiritual.

3. Building a Legacy of Faith and Generosity

The final way I want to challenge you today is to think about **the legacy you want to leave** behind. It's not just about handing down money—it's about instilling values and creating systems that will continue to impact future generations long after you're gone.

Consider:

-Leaving a portion of your wealth to charity: Whether it's your local church or a global humanitarian effort, think about how your money can continue working long after you've passed.

- Creating a family foundation: You can set up a foundation that focuses on areas you care about—education, poverty alleviation, healthcare, etc. This ensures that your wealth is used in accordance with your values and that it continues to benefit future generations.

Step-by-Step Guide to Implement

1. **Identify Your Passion Projects:** What causes stir your heart? Whether it's education, healthcare, or economic empowerment, take some time to identify what you feel passionate about. Your wealth will be much more powerful when you channel it into areas that matter to you.

2. **Start Small:** Don't think you need millions to make an impact. Even small investments can create big change. Start by contributing to a local cause or initiative.

3. **Collaborate with Others:** Team up with other like-minded people or organizations. You don't have to do this alone. By pooling resources and efforts, you can make an even greater impact.

4. **Create a Giving Plan**: Just as you plan your personal finances, plan your **giving**. Set aside a portion of your income specifically for charitable giving, and ensure that it aligns with your values.

5. **Teach Others to Give:** The best way to ensure a lasting impact is to pass on the values of generosity and stewardship to others. Encourage your family, friends, and community to join you in transforming lives and communities.

Reflection Question

How are you using your wealth to transform the world around you?

Are you investing in initiatives that will have a long-term, generational impact?

What legacy do you want to leave behind, not just for your family, but for your community and the kingdom of God?

Start thinking about these questions today. Don't wait. The time to act is now. Your wealth can change lives, and it's your responsibility to use it wisely.

Finishing Well – Living as a Testament of Faith and Financial Integrity

You've worked hard, and you've achieved a certain level of success in life. Now, as you look ahead, it's not just about building more wealth or securing your future. It's about finishing well—leaving a legacy that reflects faith, integrity, and purpose. So the question becomes: What does it mean to finish well in terms of faith and finances?

When I talk about finishing well, I'm not just talking about dying with a fat bank account. It's about living your life as a testament to faith and financial integrity. It's about making sure that your actions and choices throughout your life reflect the values you hold dear. And, if we're talking about wealth and finances, it's about ensuring that the way you've managed money speaks volumes about your character and obedience to God's principles.

So let me ask you a question right now:

What will your financial legacy say about you?

What story will your wealth tell once you've gone?

Are you living in a way that reflects God's principles of stewardship, generosity, and faithfulness?

I want you to consider these questions carefully. The way you manage your money today will shape the way others remember you. How are you showing others the importance of living with **integrity**, especially when it comes to finances?

Finishing Well: The Role of Integrity

There's a difference between success and integrity. Anyone can amass wealth, but not everyone can say that they did it with honesty, faith, and God's principles at the center of it all. As believers, our calling is not just to succeed in the world's eyes but to finish well, making sure that we are doing things in a way that honors God.

Let me give you a powerful scripture to think about. Proverbs 10:9 says, *"Whoever walks in integrity walks securely, but whoever takes crooked paths will be found out."* When you walk in integrity, you don't have to worry about hiding anything. Your life is open to scrutiny because it is marked by honesty, righteousness, and faith. The path is secure, and your legacy is strong.

I WANT YOU TO THINK about this:

How do you handle your finances in a way that speaks to your character?

Do you make choices that reflect honesty, transparency, and fairness?

Are your financial dealings consistent with your faith?

It's one thing to talk about faith; it's another to live it out. That's where integrity comes in. If you're building wealth or planning for the future, your faith should influence every decision you make—from your investments to your savings, from your business dealings to your charitable giving. Your financial decisions should be a reflection of your deep belief in God's provision and your commitment to stewarding the resources He has entrusted to you.

Living as a Testament of Faith

The world will tell you that money is for personal enjoyment, self-promotion, and luxury. But we know the truth is different. Wealth is a tool to serve others, to bless your family, and to advance the kingdom of God.

In Matthew 6:19-21, Jesus tells us, *"Do not store up for yourselves treasures on earth, where moths and vermin destroy, and where thieves break in and steal. But store up for yourselves treasures in heaven, where moths and vermin do not destroy, and where thieves do not break in and steal. For where your treasure is, there your heart will be also."* This scripture is a powerful reminder that we are not called to live for earthly wealth. Our hearts should be set on things above, where our true treasures lie.

Let me ask you—where is your treasure? Where do you put your time, energy, and resources? Are you building wealth only for yourself, or are you using your resources to make an eternal difference?

You have a responsibility to use your wealth in a way that reflects your faith. Think about how your wealth can be used to build the kingdom of God, serve others, and invest in eternal treasures. Finishing well means that your money becomes a means of honoring God and furthering His purposes.

The Importance of Generosity in Finishing Well

Proverbs 3:9-10 says, *"Honor the Lord with your wealth, with the firstfruits of all your crops; then your barns will be filled to overflowing, and your vats will brim over with new wine."* The principle here is simple: When you honor God with your wealth, He will bless you abundantly. Generosity is an essential part of finishing well.

Generosity is not just about giving a portion of your wealth; it's about having a mindset that says, "Everything I have belongs to God, and I am merely a steward." This is why charitable giving is so important. They remind us that we're not the owners of our wealth but the stewards. Giving honors God and allows us to partner with Him in His work on earth.

Here's the thing: Your generosity speaks volumes about your faith. When you give with a cheerful heart, you're not just helping others—you're building a legacy that reflects your commitment to God's kingdom. You're showing others that wealth is a tool, not a god.

So, let me ask you this—how are you giving to others? Are you generous with your wealth? Are you investing in others, whether it's through charitable giving, supporting ministries, or helping those in need? Your generosity is a key part of finishing well.

Step-by-Step Guide to Implement

1. Commit to Integrity in All Financial Dealings: Start by making a decision to conduct your finances with honesty, transparency, and fairness. This means no shortcuts, no shady deals. Treat people the way you would want to be treated in business or personal dealings. Don't compromise your integrity for money.

2. Prioritize Eternal Treasures: Evaluate where you're investing your time, money, and energy. Are you focused on things that will last forever? Think about ways you can invest in eternal treasures—things that build God's kingdom. This could mean giving to the church, supporting missions, or funding educational projects that make a difference for generations.

3. Live a Generous Life: Make giving a regular part of your life. Don't wait until you have more money. Start where you are, and be consistent. Whether it's tithing to your church, supporting a local charity, or helping someone in need, make generosity a priority.

4. Teach Others to Do the Same: Pass on the values of financial integrity and generosity to the next generation. Whether it's your children, employees, or community members, teach them the importance of handling money wisely and with a heart of giving. Leave a legacy of faith that will continue to impact others long after you're gone.

5. Review and Reflect Regularly: Take time regularly to reflect on how you're managing your wealth. Are you still on track with your goals? Are you being faithful with what God has given you? Regular reflection keeps you aligned with your purpose and ensures that your wealth is being used for good.

REFLECTION QUESTION

What will your financial legacy say about your faith and integrity?
Are you living in a way that reflects God's values in your finances?

How can you use your wealth to finish well, not just for yourself but for the generations to come?

Take some time to think about these questions. Don't rush through it—this is about setting a course for your future, making sure that you are leaving behind a legacy of faith, financial integrity, and generosity. It's time to finish well, and that starts today.

Faith in Action

Now, I challenge you to take the following actions:

- Make a decision today to live with integrity in your finances. This may mean making changes in the way you do business or the way you handle money.

- Start giving generously. Pick a cause or person in need and commit to being a consistent giver.

-Teach others the importance of financial integrity. Start with your children or the young people in your life and pass on the principles of stewardship, generosity, and faithfulness.

Remember, finishing well is about living a life that honors God, leaving a legacy that reflects your faith, your values, and your commitment to His kingdom. It's not about wealth for wealth's sake—it's about wealth that serves a greater purpose. Let's finish well, together.

Chapter 6

Harnessing Technology for Wealth Building

In today's fast-paced world, technology has unlocked countless opportunities to build wealth. What once took years to accumulate—whether it was starting a business or creating multiple streams of income—can now be done with just a **laptop** or a **smartphone**. Technology has made wealth-building more accessible than ever before, and it's time we, as believers, use it to our advantage, especially the younger generation who have grown up in this digital age.

The digital world is full of opportunities, and if we approach it with faith, integrity, and wisdom, we can use these platforms not only for personal gain but for the glory of God's kingdom. In this chapter, we'll explore some of the most effective passive income strategies available today, giving young people the tools they need to start building wealth.

Let's start by asking ourselves:

How can we leverage technology to create sustainable wealth while honoring God in the process?

The Role of Technology in Wealth Creation

Technology has completely transformed the way we live, work, and even build wealth. The internet has democratized opportunities, making it easier for anyone, anywhere, to start a business, invest, or create content that generates income.

It's no longer necessary to work a 9-5 job just to survive. Thanks to the **internet** and **technology,** there are countless ways to build wealth passively. Passive income refers to money earned with little to no ongoing effort. These income streams are essential for creating financial freedom because they allow you to earn money even when you're not actively working.

As believers, we can be wise stewards of our time and resources, using technology to build wealth in a way that honors God. Ephesians 5:15-16 reminds us to, *"Be very careful, then, how you live—not as unwise but as wise, making the most of every opportunity, because the days are evil."*

Passive Income Strategies for the Digital Age

1. Affiliate Marketing

One of the most popular and accessible ways to build passive income today is through affiliate marketing. In affiliate marketing, you promote products or services, and when someone makes a purchase through your unique affiliate link, you earn a commission. It's one of the easiest ways to get started online because you don't have to create your own products. All you need is an audience, a website, or a social media following.

For believers, affiliate marketing provides an opportunity to share faith-based products or resources with others, while earning income in the process. It's essential to ensure that the products or services you promote align with your values and will benefit your audience. There are plenty of Christian affiliate programs where you can promote books, courses, or faith-based materials.

Faith in Action: Start by identifying products or services that resonate with your beliefs. Build a platform (a blog, YouTube channel, or Instagram account) to promote these products. Keep your content authentic, and remember that your credibility is a reflection of your faith.

2. Digital Products and E-Courses

Another powerful way to generate passive income is by creating digital products. These can range from e-books to online courses. If you have knowledge or expertise in a certain area, you can package it into a product and sell it online. This strategy works particularly well for those who have skills to teach or a message to share.

For young believers, creating an online course about faith, entrepreneurship, or personal growth could be a rewarding way to generate income while serving others. Once created, the product can be sold repeatedly with minimal ongoing effort.

Faith in Action: Consider your skills and passions. What knowledge can you share with others? What problems can you solve? Build a simple online course or write an e-book to get started.

3. **Print on Demand (POD)**

If you have a flair for design, print-on-demand can be a great way to earn passive income. With POD, you create custom designs for t-shirts, mugs, and other merchandise, and when someone makes a purchase, the product is printed and shipped directly to the customer. You don't have to handle inventory, and you earn money without having to do much beyond creating the designs.

You could focus on creating faith-based designs or inspirational messages that align with your beliefs. You can even create any beautiful designs that people would love to have. POD platforms like Printful and Teespring allow you to design and sell products online with minimal effort.

Faith in Action: Start designing faith-inspired apparel or merchandise. Use your creative abilities to inspire and encourage others. Build a brand around your values and share your faith through your designs.

4. **Stock Photography**

If you are a photographer or have a passion for taking pictures, you can sell your photos on stock photography websites. Once uploaded, these images can be purchased by businesses, bloggers, or creators, providing you with a steady stream of income.

For believers, stock photography can be a way to create images that reflect your faith or cultural values. Whether it's images of nature, families, or religious symbols, there's a demand for high-quality photos across multiple industries.

Faith in Action: Start uploading your photos to stock photography sites. Focus on capturing images that tell a story of faith and hope. Be intentional about the message you are conveying through your photos.

5. **Real Estate Crowdfunding**

Another technology-driven passive income opportunity is real estate crowdfunding. With real estate crowdfunding, you can invest in properties without needing a large upfront investment. Platforms like Fundrise and RealtyMogul allow individuals to invest in real estate projects with as little as

$500. Over time, as properties generate rental income or are sold, you earn a return on your investment.

Real estate is a powerful way to build wealth over the long term, and it's becoming more accessible with technology. You don't have to be a millionaire to get started—crowdfunding has lowered the barriers to entry.

Faith in Action: Research real estate crowdfunding platforms and start investing in properties that align with your values. Diversify your investments, and remember that real estate can be a long-term way to build wealth.

6. **YouTube and Content Creation**

For those who are comfortable in front of a camera, creating content on YouTube is an excellent passive income strategy. Through YouTube, you can monetize your videos via ads, sponsorships, and affiliate links. The key is to create high-quality, engaging content that resonates with your audience.

As believers, YouTube offers an incredible platform to share faith-centered content—whether it's Bible studies, motivational talks, or lifestyle vlogs that reflect Christian values. If you have a message to share, this is a great way to make it heard.

Faith in Action: Start by creating a YouTube channel and decide what content you will focus on. Stay true to your faith, and use your platform to inspire and uplift others.

How I Attained Financial Independence

Attaining financial freedom wasn't a simple or quick journey, but every step of the way I trusted God, leaned on His wisdom, and worked diligently towards my goals. Today, I want to open up about how I attained this freedom, the strategies I used, and how you can follow in my footsteps, especially with the tools and opportunities available to us today.

It all began when I recognized that financial freedom was not just about having money—it was about having the ability to live on my own terms, with time and energy to serve God, my family, and my community. For me, this freedom began with eBook writing and branched out into multiple streams of income. Each step required faith, consistency, and a willingness to learn.

Let me share how I got here.

1. Ebook Writing: The Cornerstone of My Journey

The first step on my path to financial freedom was writing **eBooks**. I had always been passionate about sharing knowledge, and writing seemed like the perfect way to do that. But what set me apart was my focus on creating value for others. Instead of writing just any book, I chose topics that aligned with my own experiences and expertise—topics that would help others grow, financially and spiritually. As a matter of fact I later ventured to writing on various niches ensuring that my content either solves a problem or add much value to my target audience.

What worked for me was focusing on niche markets areas where there was a demand but not too much competition. Writing these books became a way to not just make money, but to serve people with practical advice that could change their lives. As I built my portfolio, I quickly realized how passive income could start flowing in, even when I wasn't actively working.

I took advantage of platforms like Amazon Kindle Direct Publishing (KDP) and Draft2Digital to publish my eBooks. These platforms allowed me to publish and market my books to a global audience with minimal effort. Once the books were written and published, I didn't have to keep working on them to earn money. The key here was scaling. I didn't stop at one book. I wrote multiple eBooks, each serving a unique purpose, which helped me build a sustainable income stream.

2. Ghostwriting: Turning My Words into Other People's Success

As I gained more experience in writing, I discovered ghostwriting—a service where I wrote books or articles for others, but they took the credit. At first, it felt a little strange not getting the recognition for my work, but then I realized the opportunity that came with it: earning without the need for personal recognition. Ghostwriting allowed me to take my writing skills to a professional level, and it paid well.

I started by offering ghostwriting services to individuals looking to publish books but who either didn't have the time or the skills to do it themselves. Ghostwriting became one of my most lucrative ventures. With the skills I had developed in writing and the connections I made, I was able to charge premium rates for my work. Upwork and Fiverr became my go-to platforms to find clients looking for high-quality ghostwriters.

Over time, I built a reputation for myself, and my ghostwriting career flourished. Writing for others allowed me to use my creativity to impact lives in ways I couldn't have imagined—because the books I wrote were often life-changing for the readers who didn't know I existed.

3. Freelancing on Fiverr and Upwork: Turning Skills Into Money

After gaining experience in eBook writing and ghostwriting, I moved into freelancing on Fiverr and Upwork. Both platforms allowed me to use my skills to generate consistent income from a variety of projects. Whether it was writing content, creating marketing strategies, freelancing opened up doors for me that I never thought possible.

What I loved most about freelancing was the flexibility. It allowed me to choose the work that fit my skill set and work schedule. With Fiverr, I was able to offer specific services such as content writing, book editing, and even social media management. On Upwork, I expanded my reach even further, working on larger projects like ghostwriting books or doing marketing consulting for businesses.

Both platforms allowed me to leverage the skills I already had, and the more I delivered, the more clients I gained. Eventually, my freelancing turned into a full-fledged business, and I started earning thousands a month from my freelance projects alone.

Faith in Action: If freelancing is something you're interested in, here's a simple guide to get started:

1. Identify your skills—what services can you offer to others?
2. Set up your profile—whether on Fiverr, Upwork, or another platform, create a profile that highlights your skills.
3. Start small—take on small projects to build your reputation and earn reviews.
4. Over-deliver—always give more than what is expected to build client trust.

---

4. Affiliate Marketing: Sharing Products and Earning Passive Income

ONE OF THE MOST POWERFUL ways I achieved financial freedom was through affiliate marketing. This was the game-changer for me because it allowed me to promote products I loved and earn commissions without having to create them myself. It was a perfect match with my philosophy of passive income.

Affiliate marketing became an integral part of my online income streams. By joining affiliate programs like Amazon Associates, I was able to promote books, courses, and even software tools that I personally believed in. The key to success in affiliate marketing is trust. I didn't just promote anything; I focused on products that I truly used and knew would benefit my audience.

I promoted these products and the more value I provided through my content, the more trust I earned—and the more commissions I earned as a result.

Faith in Action: Here's how you can get started with affiliate marketing:

1. Join affiliate programs that resonate with your audience and values.

2. Create content that educates and promotes these products without being pushy.

3. Use your platforms—whether a blog, YouTube, or social media, promote your affiliate links in a way that provides value.

4. Be patient—affiliate marketing takes time, but consistency pays off.

---

5. Forex Trading: The Latest Addition to My Wealth-Building Portfolio

CURRENTLY, I'VE ADDED **Forex trading** to my wealth-building journey. While this may seem intimidating at first, I've learned that **Forex trading** can be an incredible way to earn passive income with the right strategies. I took time to educate myself, practice, and learn from other successful traders. Over time, I've built a solid trading plan and developed a disciplined approach that has led to consistent profits.

Forex trading allows me to leverage market movements to generate income passively, as long as I'm following my trading strategy and sticking to my rules. Like any form of investing, it requires patience, discipline, and research, but it's proven to be a powerful tool in my wealth-building toolkit.

Faith in Action: Here's how to get started with Forex trading:

1. Educate yourself—learn the basics of Forex trading and study the market.

2. Create a trading plan—have a strategy before you begin trading.

3. Practice with a demo account—most platforms offer a demo account to practice without risking real money.

4. Invest wisely—start with small amounts and grow as you learn.

Attaining financial freedom isn't a one-size-fits-all journey, and it's important to remember that success is not instant. Every step I took, from eBook writing to Forex trading, involved faith, action, and God's guidance. I didn't rush the process; instead, I trusted the journey, knowing that each income stream was a tool God gave me to serve others.

It is my hope that you are encouraged to take that first step, whether it's writing an eBook, starting a freelance career, or learning how to trade. Don't be afraid to start small, but start now. God will meet you where you are and help you grow.

Reflection Question

Are you ready to take the first step towards financial freedom?

What can you do today to begin your journey?

The Need for Mentorship on the Path to Financial Freedom

When I reflect on the journey that led me to financial freedom, there's one key factor that stands out above everything else: mentorship. Yes, I had faith, I had the drive, and I had the resources, but it was the wisdom of others—those who had walked the path before me—that made all the difference. I could never have achieved all that I have today without the guidance and insight of people who believed in me and my potential.

Whether you're trying to grow a business, learn a new skill, or achieve financial freedom, the value of a mentor cannot be overstated. A mentor is someone who has been where you are now, and can guide you through the pitfalls, missteps, and mistakes they once made. Their experiences are golden and can save you years of trial and error.

Let me explain why mentorship has been a game-changer for me and how you can benefit from it in your own journey.

1. <u>Mentorship Shortens the Learning Curve</u>

When I first ventured into writing eBooks, I had no idea what I was doing. Sure, I had the motivation and the drive, but I didn't have the knowledge of the best platforms for self-publishing, how to market my books, or even the nuances of crafting a compelling eBook that would resonate with readers. I could've spent years learning by trial and error, but I didn't have to. I found mentors—successful self-publishers—who showed me the ropes, answered my questions, and gave me the tools I needed to succeed faster.

They helped me understand the importance of choosing a niche, how to create a compelling title, and how to craft a professional-looking cover. They also helped me learn how to market my books effectively, leveraging tools I would never have known about. With the right mentorship, I was able to avoid common mistakes, saving me valuable time and money.

Faith in Action

- Find a mentor who is already successful in the area you want to grow in, whether it's financial freedom, business growth, or personal development.

- Ask for guidance. Don't be afraid to reach out—people who have succeeded are often willing to help others along the way.

2. <u>Accountability and Encouragement</u>

It's easy to get discouraged along the journey, especially when things don't go as planned. Whether it's slow sales on your first eBook, dead-end freelance projects or losing money in Forex trading, the path to financial freedom is filled with setbacks.

During these moments, having a mentor who has been through similar challenges and can offer accountability is crucial. A mentor isn't just someone who offers advice—they push you to keep going, to keep moving forward, and to believe in yourself when you want to quit.

I can't count the number of times I wanted to give up during tough times, but my mentors kept encouraging me. They reminded me of the bigger picture, of the goals I had set, and most importantly, of the faith I had in God's plan for my life. Without that accountability, I might have stopped before I even got started.

Faith in Action

- If you already have a mentor, set up regular check-ins to ensure accountability.

- If you don't, find someone who is further ahead on their journey, and ask them to keep you accountable to your goals.

-Pray for guidance in finding the right mentor.

3. <u>Learning from Experience</u>

There's a profound difference between learning something from a book or a course and learning from someone who has already lived through the experience. Mentors provide a wealth of practical wisdom that you can't find in textbooks or online articles.

For example, as I grew in affiliate marketing, I encountered pitfalls and challenges that could've easily derailed my success. But I had a mentor in affiliate marketing who had already faced those challenges and shared their experience with me. They told me what worked, what didn't, and how to optimize my campaigns.

Instead of wasting time experimenting with different strategies on my own, I was able to implement the advice from my mentor right away and start seeing results. Learning from someone's firsthand experiences is invaluable because it equips you to handle challenges in a way that's much more efficient and less painful.

Faith in Action

- Look for a mentor who has the type of experience you want to gain. They don't have to have the same exact path, but they must be experienced in your area of interest.

- Learn from their mistakes—don't repeat them.

- Ask questions that will help you avoid common pitfalls.

4. <u>Wisdom Beyond Knowledge</u>

A mentor isn't just someone who shares knowledge with you—they also impart wisdom. Knowledge is helpful, but wisdom is what helps you apply that knowledge in real-life situations.

Take, for example, Forex trading. I could've learned all the technical analysis and trading strategies on my own, but my mentor in this field taught me something even more valuable—the mindset required for successful trading. They taught me that trading isn't just about following a system; it's about discipline, patience, and emotional control. That kind of wisdom can't be taught through books—it has to be passed down through experience.

This wisdom helped me approach my trades with a clear mind and avoid making emotional decisions that would have cost me money. It also helped me build my financial mindset—understanding that making money requires a long-term view, not quick wins.

Faith in Action

- Don't just seek out someone to teach you the "how-to's"; look for someone who will teach you how to think.

- As you learn, ask your mentor questions that will develop your wisdom and mindset.

- Incorporate what you've learned into your daily actions.

---

5. The Power of Giving Back

As I gained success in my financial journey, one thing became clear: mentorship is a two-way street. The mentors who helped me along the way didn't just give out of kindness—they also had a heart for giving back, and I've adopted the same mindset.

Mentorship doesn't end with receiving—it's about paying it forward. Once you've reached a certain level of success, I encourage you to be a mentor to others. Share your story, your experiences, and the wisdom you've gained. Helping someone else along their journey is not just about them—it's about creating a ripple effect of success and passing on the lessons that were taught to you.

One of the best ways to give back is to teach others the principles of financial freedom, so they can build their own wealth, help their families, and impact their communities.

Faith in Action

- Pay it forward: as you grow, start mentoring others.

- Share your story with those who need it. Let them know it's possible to achieve success, no matter where they start.

- Pray for opportunities to be a blessing to others through your mentorship.

The need for mentorship in your journey toward financial freedom is undeniable. No matter how much faith you have, or how hard you work, you'll need guidance along the way. A mentor can provide direction, wisdom, and accountability that will help you avoid costly mistakes and achieve your goals faster.

Reflection Question

Have you found a mentor yet? What step can you take today to start finding someone who can guide you toward your goals?

Faith in Action:

1. Pray for God's guidance to help you find the right mentor in your financial or business journey.

2. Take the initiative—don't wait for someone to approach you. Reach out to potential mentors.

3. Give back—once you've learned, be willing to mentor others and help them grow as well.

Conclusion

Living a Balanced Life—Honoring God in Faith and Finances

As we come to the end of this journey, I want to leave you with a thought that encapsulates everything we've discussed throughout the chapters of this book: True financial freedom isn't just about accumulating wealth—it's about living a life that honors God, creates a legacy, and inspires others to do the same.

The journey to financial freedom isn't just a destination; it's a lifelong journey that requires balance, discipline, and most importantly, faith. As we've explored the principles of faith and finances, I hope you've gained not only the practical tools but also the mindset and the vision necessary to live a life that balances your financial ambitions with your spiritual calling.

BUT WHAT DOES IT MEAN to live a truly balanced life?

A balanced life is one where faith and finances coexist in a way that reflects the will of God for your life. It's a life where you don't just focus on seeking wealth for yourself, but also on using your wealth to serve others, to build your family's future, to impact your community, and ultimately, to glorify God.

I know that sometimes, especially when the pressures of day-to-day survival kick in, it's easy to lose sight of this bigger picture. You get caught up in the grind and forget about the purpose behind it all. I want to encourage you, as you move forward on your journey, to keep your eyes fixed on living with purpose and living with faith. Don't get distracted by the pursuit of wealth for its own sake. Instead, focus on using your financial success as a tool to live out your God-given calling.

The Call to Live a Life of Purpose

Throughout this book, we've talked about various strategies for building wealth: writing eBooks, ghostwriting, freelancing**, **affiliate marketing, Forex trading, and so much more. These are all powerful avenues that can lead to financial success. But none of them, or any other wealth-building methods, will mean much if they don't serve a larger purpose—a purpose aligned with God's will.

You see, wealth on its own is not evil. Money in itself is not the root of all evil. It's the **love of money**—the greed and the selfishness—that can cause us to lose sight of what truly matters. But when you approach wealth-building with the right mindset, one that honors God and seeks to bless others, it becomes a tool for good—a tool for building not just your life, but the lives of others as well.

So, what does it look like to live a balanced life in terms of finances and faith?

1. **Seek God First:** Above all, put God at the center of your life. Seek His guidance in your financial decisions, and trust that He will lead you toward success when you honor Him with your finances. Matthew 6:33 reminds us, *"But seek first the kingdom of God and His righteousness, and all these things shall be added to you."* When you seek God first, everything else falls into place.

2. **Serve Others:** True financial freedom isn't about what you can accumulate for yourself, but about what you can give to others. God's word teaches us that it is more blessed to give than to receive (Acts 20:35).

3. **Live Generously:** Don't just save and hoard your money. Be a*blessing to others. We're all called to be stewards, and that means using what we have to help others. Whether it's through investing in the education of the next

generation, supporting charities, or funding kingdom work, generosity should be a lifestyle. Proverbs 11:25 tells us, "A generous person will prosper; whoever refreshes others will be refreshed."

4. **Build a Legacy:** Don't just think about yourself—think about the generations that will come after you. Create a legacy that honors God and benefits others. Your financial success should serve as a foundation upon which your children, grandchildren, and even your community can build. Think long-term, and create something that will last beyond your lifetime.

Honoring God in Your Finances

We've also talked about financial literacy, entrepreneurship, and investing. These are all important topics. But at the heart of all these strategies is the understanding that God owns everything. Psalm 24:1 reminds us, *"The earth is the Lord's, and everything in it, the world, and all who live in it."* When you realize that everything you have, including your finances, ultimately belongs to God, it changes the way you view money. It becomes less about your personal gain and more about how you can use it to honor God and impact the world around you.

This is why wealth-building is not just about accumulating—it's about managing what God has entrusted to you. That's what good stewardship is all about: managing God's resources wisely. As you continue your journey, remember that stewardship is key—it's not about how much you make, but about how wisely you manage what you have.

As you go about building your wealth and your financial future, don't forget that the ultimate goal is to glorify God. Let your success be a testimony of His faithfulness, and let your actions show others that **true wealth** is not just measured in dollars, but in the lives you've impacted along the way.

Living with Intentionality

As you take the next step on your financial journey, I want to encourage you to live with intentionality. Don't just let life happen to you—take control of your finances and your future, but always keep in mind that your wealth is not just for your own comfort and enjoyment. It's a tool to fulfill a higher calling.

- Be intentional with your money: Spend and save wisely, and make sure every dollar is working toward fulfilling your purpose.

- Be intentional with your time: Your time is just as valuable as your money. Spend it wisely, and focus on building something that will last.

- Be intentional with your relationships: Surround yourself with people who will push you to grow and challenge you to be better. And as you grow, pour into others and invest in their success too.

As you live a life that honors God and builds wealth, remember that the true measure of success is not how much you have, but what you do with what you've been given.

The Legacy You Leave

As I close, I want you to think about the legacy you will leave behind. What kind of impact will you make on your family, your community, and the world at large? What kind of difference will your life make?

Will you be remembered for your generosity, your wisdom, your faith, or the lives you touched? The choices you make today will shape the future, not just for you, but for everyone you touch. Leave a legacy that will inspire future generations to do the same—to live a life that honors God and builds others up.

If you're ready to take control of your finances, live a life of faith, and leave a legacy that will outlast you, then I invite you to take the next step. Make a commitment today to start living a life that balances faith and finances, that creates a legacy of service, and that impacts the world in a positive way.

If you need help along the way, I'm here for you. Feel free to reach out, and let's continue this journey together. My story is just one example of what is possible when you trust God, build wealth with integrity, and use your success to serve others.

Contact Details

You can reach me for mentorship, guidance, or just to connect at:

Email: gordonnsowine@gmail.com

Phone Number: +233555017768

Let's build a future of financial freedom together—a future that honors God, serves others, and leaves a lasting legacy.

Reflection

1. Poverty is not a sign of godliness, nor is wealth a measure of faith. Both are tools that can be used to honor God—how you use them matters most.

2. God does not test our faith by our financial struggles. True faith is shown through how we manage what we have, regardless of how much or how little.

3. Financial struggles do not define your worth in God's eyes. What defines you is your faithfulness, integrity, and the heart you bring to everything you do.

4. Wealth is not a curse; it's a responsibility. How we steward it—whether little or much—determines whether it serves God's purpose in our lives.

5. God desires that we live in abundance, not just spiritually but in every area of our lives, including financially. Prosperity is part of the blessings He has for us when we follow His principles.

6. Don't equate financial success with selfishness, and don't see poverty as a badge of humility. God can use both wealth and lack to shape your character and purpose.

7. Money is neither evil nor virtuous—it's simply a tool. It's how you handle it, and the purpose you use it for, that determines whether it builds you up or holds you back.

8. Being financially blessed isn't about hoarding wealth, it's about becoming a channel for blessings. Prosperity should serve the greater good, not just your own desires.

9. Faith in God doesn't mean you have to accept poverty as your fate. It means trusting God to provide, to prosper you, and to teach you how to use your resources wisely for His kingdom.

10. Wealth isn't a test of faith—it's a gift that must be managed wisely. God tests our faith through our decisions, not through our bank accounts.

11. Living a life of faith isn't about being poor or wealthy, it's about being obedient to God's will in every area, including how we manage and steward our finances.

12. God is not limited by your financial situation. Whether rich or poor, your faith should be rooted in the trust that God will guide you to success in all areas of life.

13. Abundance is not reserved for the chosen few—it's available to all who align their finances with God's principles, live generously, and steward their resources faithfully.

14. Being wealthy doesn't make you more righteous, and being poor doesn't make you more humble. It's how you handle what God gives you that counts, and how you use it to serve others.

15. Faith and finances don't live in separate worlds. A strong faith in God leads to wisdom in managing money, and this wisdom builds a foundation for lasting financial success.

Don't miss out!

Visit the website below and you can sign up to receive emails whenever GORDON MILLS publishes a new book. There's no charge and no obligation.

https://books2read.com/r/B-A-ACPUC-DZDIF

BOOKS 2 READ

Connecting independent readers to independent writers.